HAUTE-SAVOIE
&
MONT BLANC
Mountain Bike Guide

HAUTE-SAVOIE
&
MONT BLANC
Mountain Bike Guide

**Didier Cassani
Jean-Marc Lamory**

TWO WHEELS

This edition published in 1994 by

Two Wheels - an imprint of
Two Heads Publishing
12A Franklyn Suite
The Priory
Haywards Heath
West Sussex
RH16 3LB

Copyright this edition © **Two Wheels** 1994

First published by Editions Olizane SA, Geneva
Copyright original edition © Editions Olizane SA

A catalogue record for this book is available from the
British Library.

Every effort has been made to ensure the accuracy of
information in this book. Details such as Rights of Way,
tracks, roads, places to see and refreshment stops may
be subject to change and the authors and publishers
cannot accept liability for any errors or omissions.

ISBN   1-898933-10-3

Translated by Angela Parker.
Cover Design by David Spencer.
Maps by Geoff Apps.
Photographs by the authors.
Printed & bound by Caldra House Ltd., Hove, Sussex.

CONTENTS

RIDE LOCATION MAP

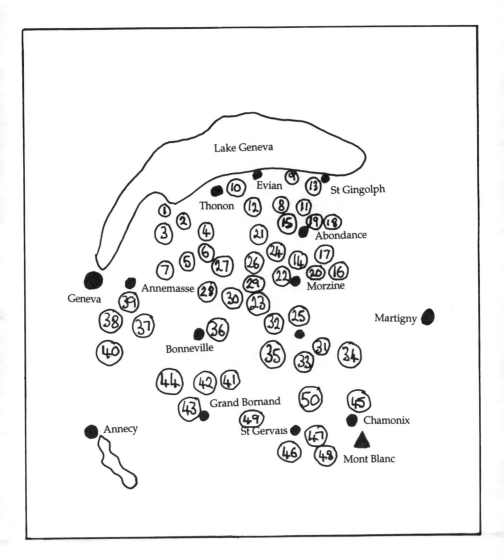

INTRODUCTION

In a region offering tremendous potential for off-road cycling, we found that there was no comprehensive guide to mountain bike routes in the area. Cyclists had to make up their own routes and many of them found this a problem, because to devise a suitable route you had to know the area and the terrain extremely well.

As we thought that most people, particularly visitors, would not have this knowledge, we decided to produce this guide to Haute-Savoie, our local region. We thought that with its large number of varied circuits it would be invaluable to all those who wish to cycle off-road.

We wanted this guide to demonstrate our complete approach to mountain biking and how we think it can be integrated with other sporting activities which respect the natural environment. It is not just a trendy sport but is a completely different kind of transport which is as useful in the valleys as on a mountain. We dislike the term 'mountain bike' because it is not the correct term; this type of bike can be used anywhere - on the flat, on mountains, on forest tracks. Mountain bikes simply enable you to cover long distances over areas where it would be tiresome to walk. Nevertheless, mountain biking is only appropriate on suitable terrain - it would be foolhardy to undertake steep descents on bumpy terrain or uneven paths on anything other than a bike suitable for that purpose. So the knowledge of, and choice of terrain, are all important.

The physical and technical characteristics of mountain biking have also made the sport more widespread. Off-road cycling is demanding, on occasions you have to push yourself further than you believed possible. It does not just do you good physically, it does you good mentally as well. It is up to you to discover your own limits, and when you get the balance right your trips will become particularly enjoyable.

A good cycling technique is particularly important over difficult terrain. Good technique basically comprises learning to reduce your weight on the front wheel, to know where to put the wheel, to pedal at the right time, to correctly position your body, to avoid skidding, or, where necessary, to know how to lock the wheels in a controlled drift; fundamentally it means being at one with your bike.

Nature, discovery, contemplation, escape, challenge, fresh air and a glow of well-being are some of the first words which spring to mind when trying to describe mountain biking. These feelings will strike a cord with all people who enjoy outdoor pursuits because they coincide with their fundamental needs. Cycling off-road in Haute-Savoie is a fantastic way of satisfying these needs.

It is for this reason that we do not recognise and would never recognise the so-called mountain bikers who practise their sport like fleeing hordes and who soon ruin their chosen area. Not content with ruining the countryside they also manage to annoy walkers, ramblers and farmers, who as a consequence see a potential enemy in every mountain biker.

So in order that we can continue to cycle wherever we like please respect the environment and learn to ride in harmony with other users of our beautiful countryside.

We wanted to offer the broadest possible choice of routes in Haute-Savoie and even a bit beyond. For this reason you will find rides in relatively unknown areas, but these are particularly suitable for mountain biking. For practical reasons we have divided the region into nine areas which mainly stand alone geographically or have distinct mountain ranges.

Finally, we have striven to offer the greatest choice of routes in terms of length and technical difficulty. But we want this guide to apply equally to those who are out for a family jaunt, to beginners looking to develop their skills, and to the toughies to whom we offer high climbs, often long and more technically difficult.

Of course, this guide is still just a selection of possible rides, and as such the selection is always up for discussion. However, we decided to fill the gap for those looking for information. Our choice has been guided by the objectives explained above, by our own knowledge, and by the information which we were kindly given. The circuits we have described are not an exhaustive list of this area's possibilities but they still offer you a considerable choice which will offer a new perspective on Haute-Savoie, and open up new experiences.

Haute-Savoie

Skiing in the winter and superb alpine walking and cycling in the summer is what Haute-Savoie has to offer. It is a beautiful region, covered by forest, known as much for the mountains in the centre and south as for the lush, gentle countryside south of Lake Geneva (*Lac Léman*), in the area of Chablais. The natural splendour is enhanced by attractive alpine villages.

Summer is the best time to enjoy all the rides in this book, although the low-level routes will remain accessible in the spring and onset of winter when there is a likelihood of snow on the mountains blocking some routes. Summer temperatures are generally warmer than those experienced in the UK, although these are mitigated by altitude.

There is no shortage of accommodation in the region. Many of the resorts are geared for the skiing season, and some hotels close for a break from September to December to prepare themselves for winter. There is a rare delight in visiting a skiing area off-season. Late summer is often the best time as the majority of summer visitors have departed, the main facilities are generally still operating, and you feel a curious sense of freedom with seemingly having mountain trails to yourself.

How to get there

We feel that this book will be used mainly by two groups of people. One, people who are on holiday in the area and wish to go out cycling. Two, experienced cyclists and mountain bike riders who want to travel to the area to enjoy a cycling holiday. For the first group, detailed information on how to get to Haute-Savoie will be superfluous as they will already be there! For the second group, we won't apologise for not giving you chapter and verse on travelling to Haute-Savoie from the UK as we reckon that if you're capable of planning an off-road cycling holiday then you are more than capable of finding your way to the area.

To place yourself in a position from where you can easily reach the majority of rides in this book it is best to choose somewhere central. All Haute-Savoie is within 40 miles of Geneva and from there you can travel by train to Thonon-les-Bains on the shore of Lake Geneva, and then south by road into the heart of the region, towards Morzine. Trains also go east to Cluses, via Annemasse, to give similar access to the area around Morzine but from the south. You can continue by train from Cluses to Chamonix and Mont Blanc, via St Gervais and les Houches.

TGV trains operate from Paris to Annecy, to Geneva (for Thonon les Bains and Evian), to Cluses (for Morzine and Taninges), and to St Gervais (for Chamonix).

If you prefer to put your bikes on the car rack, it is around 550 miles to the heart of Haute-Savoie, from the Channel ports, and a good 10 hour drive.

Didier Cassani & Jean-Marc Lamory

HOW TO USE THIS GUIDE

Choosing a route

We cannot stress too much the importance of being cautious in your choice of route, particularly if you are a beginner. Start with the easier routes. In order to do this, consult the Ride Reference Tables and the descriptions, which clearly show the distance, the gradient, the rating and the time needed. It is much better to underestimate your capabilities and enjoy yourself on an easy route than to overdo it. Use the Ride Reference Tables to select rides by region, difficulty or distance.

On some of the rides you can reach the start by using a ski-lift, and many rides have a ski-lift nearby which could be used to gain height initially or to vary the route without cycling all the way. Mountain bikes are available for hire by the day or week almost anywhere suitably interesting enough to merit using one. All this information can be found in the Ride Information Table.

You must be aware that the state of the terrain (wet or dry), and the weather, have enormous bearings on the technical and physical difficulties. It is easy to check the weather conditions and the forecast with the local information centres. Training and fitness is, of course, vital. There is no point in embarking on a long and difficult journey if you have not touched a bike for months. All the above is common sense but worth remembering.

Ride Reference Tables

There are four Ride Reference Tables. Each one shows the ride number, the name, the overall rating, the distance, the region and the page number in the book. They are designed to make it easy to choose a route.

Region & Number

At a glance you can see all the rides in a particular region.

Rating

All the rides are listed by overall rating, from one star * to four stars ****. Please see below for details of how the rides are rated.

Distance

Details of all the rides can be seen in distance order. Particularly useful if time, and therefore distance, is your main criteria for selecting a ride.

Information

Details of where to hire a bike, the telephone number of the local information centre, routes with a ski-lift which can be used to reach the start, routes with a ski-lift nearby.

Assessing the rides

Once you have chosen a likely route look at that individual ride description for a more detailed assessment. Because of the broad range of its routes, this guide is equally applicable to beginners and experienced riders. We have therefore tried to give the maximum amount of information on each route in the facts table at the start of each ride description. The ratings range from one star * to four stars **** and the individual ride facts table shows at a glance the overall difficulty of any given route, under the headings of duration, overall rating, terrain and effort.

Duration

The routes vay from 1 to in excess of 4 hours although it is stressed that this is an average time only which will vary with the fitness of the rider, the weather conditions and how many stops you choose to make.

Overall rating

This is an overall rating for the route and combines the average duration, the nature of the terrain, obstacles, technical difficulties, and physical effort required. One star * routes are easy and accessible to all with good basic fitness. Two stars ** are for more sporty mountain bikers. Three stars *** for dedicated and fit riders. Four stars **** are testing routes for experienced off-roaders.

Terrain

This indicates the type of surface you will be cycling on. One star * routes are on small tarmac lanes, tracks or well maintained pistes, with no technical difficulties. Two stars ** will add sometimes narrow and uneven paths, for those with basically sound technique. Three stars *** covers routes which may offer a broad range of terrain with difficult sections requiring technical competence. On four star **** routes the terrain may in parts be barely passable (involving actual carrying of bikes).

Effort

This is a guide, in the broadest sense, to the overall physical effort required. One star * needs little physical effort for someone in reasonable physical condition. Two stars ** will at times require a certain amount of effort Three star *** routes are demanding and are for riders who enjoy physical exertion. Four stars **** are for the super fit.

Ride descriptions

All the essential details on the ride can be found in the facts box at the start of each ride description. This shows the start & finish point, the distance, the climb, the duration, and the ratings - overall, terrain, effort. Also shown is the number of the relevant IGN map and details of general access to the area of the ride. Each route is described succinctly but with all the necessary information. The length of the description does not relate to the length of the route; thus, a straightforward long run, or an obvious path are described briefly whereas other paths or routes with a need for more directions are described in greater detail.

Sketch maps

The sketch maps are drawn from IGN (*Institut Géographique National*) maps, the French equivalent of Ordnance Survey maps, available at scales of 1:50000 and 1:25000. The sketches are accurate, but obviously simplified. You will find the main roads, mountain peaks, ridges, cols (passes), forests (dotted areas), and height points(in metres). The actual route is marked by a dashed line. The most important place names and landmarks are also shown to enable you to check your route. However, these sketch maps are only a guide to the route and you should use the relevant IGN French map to undertake your trip. Once you have chosen your route you should obtain the relevant IGN 1:25000 map and mark the outline sketch on it, then you will have enough information to follow the route accurately and undertake detours should you wish to add to or shorten the ride.

Waymarks

The route is likely to be marked by various signposts and waymarks that could be from numerous sources; national or local footpaths, skiing pistes, local mountain biking circuits. A mixture of too many signs can be confusing so it is better not to place too much trust in them unless we state otherwise. Signs showing place names and directions are more reliable and will enable you to orientate yourself more accurately.

Variations

By all means take our basic routes and expand them, but be careful in your planning, refer to the map and make sure the route you are planning is suited to both your capabilities and your mode of transport. Obviously it is possible to combine and vary routes and we have outlined a few suggestions where this is particularly appropriate.

BE PREPARED

Route Difficulty
The climb and the distance are given for each ride. They are totally objective because they are measurable. We also give an overall difficulty rating for each route; a rating for the nature of the terrain; an effort rating, considering the physical and technical difficulties. We have taken a great deal of care in our advice, but they are personal interpretations and obviously subjective. So it is best to treat the advice cautiously, and at first be prudent in your choice of routes until you are sure you can interpret our method of assessment.

Seasons
The summer and fine days are obviously best for mountain biking, certainly in Haute-Savoie, where heavy snowfalls make many of our routes impassable in winter and spring. However, it seems short-sighted to restrict mountain biking to the summer as Haute-Savoie offers varied terrain and we are sure that whatever the season, you will find a route that suits you in this guide. Whether it is early winter or spring many rides will remain accessible provided that snow has not reached the valleys. So be sure to enjoy these 'in between' seasons. Really, it is a question of the terrain. Provided the ground remains passable, the season does not really matter.

Equipment
Helmet and gloves are the basic necessities for safety. Also a large bottle of high energy drink and snacks. Cyclists' shorts and mountain biking shoes also aid comfort. Other clothes should be adapted to the weather conditions, to the altitude and the length of the journey. It is also a good idea to take all-weather garments as taking too much, with room to store discarded clothing, is always better than not taking enough. To this end, a small rucksack would be most useful. Don't forget the sunglasses.

The Bike
Given the extreme conditions to which your bike may be subjected, it is essential that you check it is well maintained before embarking on a journey.
  As a general rule, check the state and pressure of your tyres, the wear and the optimum position of the brake blocks, the tightness of the steering column,

the gears and gear levers (going up and down through the gears), and the lubrication of the chain, gears and other cables. However good the state of your bike a repair kit can be most useful, especially if a puncture occurs a long way from home.

The kit should contain as a minimum: a bicycle pump, an inner tube, a breakdown kit, glue, a puncture repair kit, two tyre levers, an all-in-one tool, and finally a spare chain link. Check that the pump has an adequately sized valve.

Technique

The following advice on riding your bike may enable you to enjoy your trip with greater confidence, especially in alpine conditions.

On the ascent, adhesion and propulsion are the key words. Therefore, select the right gear before attacking the slope, having already assessed the terrain. To give the back wheel the maximum grip, climb staying in the saddle (position yourself so as not to allow the front wheel to rise up). The design of the back tyre is also an important element in speed and grip; a deep tread will allow you to refine your performance on the ascents. When the steepness of the slope really becomes too much, do not be afraid to get off and push!

On the descent, be cautious. In all cases, and especially when the slope becomes increasingly steep, lower your saddle and transfer your weight to the back by leaning backwards (your should not rest on the saddle). Hold the handlebars firmly so that you are in total control of your descent, especially on rocky ground. Position your feet so that the pedals are level (horizontal), brake with both brakes (lead with the back brake and at the same time use the front in order to completely control your speed).

If you hire a bike locally, ensure that you familiarise yourself with it before heading to the hills.

REGION & NUMBER
RIDE REFERENCE TABLE

NO	RIDE	RATING	KM	REGION	PAGE
1	Lake Geneva (Yvoire-Sciez)	*	9	Bas Chablais	29
2	Lake Geneva (Sciez-Allinges)	*	11	Bas Chablais	31
3	Mont de Boisy	**	7	Bas Chablais	34
4	La Boucle des Allinges	**	17	Bas Chablais	36
5	Tete de Char (Targaillon)	**	14	Bas Chablais	38
6	Mont Forchat	**	15	Bas Chablais	40
7	Signal des Voirons	***	15	Bas Chablais	43
8	The Gavot Plain 1	*	11	Plateau du Gavot	48
9	Haut-Leman	*	18	Plateau du Gavot	50
10	Marin	**	14	Plateau du Gavot	53
11	From Bernex to Vinzier	**	20	Plateau du Gavot	56
12	The Gavot Plain 2	**	25	Plateau du Gavot	59
13	Pic des Memises	***	15	Plateau du Gavot	62
14	Lac des Plagnes	**	14	Val d'Abondance	66
15	Centfontaines	**	16	Val d'Abondance	68
16	Champery	***	16	Val d'Abondance	71
17	The tour of Grincheux	***	19	Val d'Abondance	74
18	A tour of Mont Chauffe	***	19	Val d'Abondance	76
19	Chalets d'Autigny	***	25	Val d'Abondance	78
20a	Les cretes de Super Morzine	*	3.5	Vallee d'Aulps	82
20b	Les cretes de Super Morzine	*	7	Vallee d'Aulps	82
20c	Les cretes de Super Morzine	*	8	Vallee d'Aulps	82
21	Drouzin - Le Mont	*	8.5	Vallee d'Aulps	85
22	Les Lindarets	*	17	Vallee d'Aulps	87
23	The tour of Chery	**	11	Vallee d'Aulps	90
24	The Vallee d'Aulps	**	16	Vallee d'Aulps	92
25	Pointe de la Turche	**	17	Vallee d'Aulps	95
26	Saint-Jean d'Aulps	****	17	Vallee d'Aulps	97
27	Tour of La Pointe de Mirabel	*	8	Vallee Verte	102
28	Le Bachais	*	13	Vallee Verte	104

REGION & NUMBER
RIDE REFERENCE TABLE

NO	RIDE	RATING	KM	REGION	PAGE
29	Petetoz	**	7	Vallee Verte	106
30	La Haute Pointe	***	15	Vallee Verte	108
31	Samoens - Sixt	*	11	Vallee du Giffre	112
32	Plateau de Loex	*	12	Vallee du Giffre	114
33	Lac de Gers	**	14	Vallee du Giffre	117
34	Sixt - Fer a Cheval	**	16	Vallee du Giffre	119
35	Les Carroz	**	21	Vallee du Giffre	121
36	A tour of Mole	***	11	Vallee du Giffre	123
37	La Chapelle Rambaud	*	16	Saleve	126
38	Le Saleve 1	**	8	Saleve	129
39	Le Saleve 2	**	12	Saleve	131
40	Groisy - Villy Le Bouveret	**	12	Saleve	133
41	Les Fretes	**	8	Bornes & Aravis	138
42	Col des Annes	***	26	Bornes & Aravis	140
43	Lac de Lessy	****	13	Bornes & Aravis	143
44	Petit-Bornand	****	33	Bornes & Aravis	145
45	Chamonix (Bois du Bouchet)	*	15	Mont Blanc	150
46	Le Bettex	**	11	Mont Blanc	152
47	Col de Voza	***	22	Mont Blanc	155
48	Bionnassay	***	10	Mont Blanc	158
49	Chalet de Mayeres	***	10	Mont Blanc	160
50	Lac de Pormenaz	***	18	Mont Blanc	162

RATING
RIDE REFERENCE TABLE

NO	RIDE	RATING	KM	REGION	PAGE
1	Lake Geneva (Yvoire-Sciez)	*	9	Bas Chablais	29
2	Lake Geneva (Sciez-Allinges)	*	11	Bas Chablais	31
8	The Gavot Plain 1	*	11	Plateau du Gavot	48
9	Haut-Leman	*	18	Plateau du Gavot	50
20a	Les cretes de Super Morzine	*	3.5	Vallee d'Aulps	82
20b	Les cretes de Super Morzine	*	7	Vallee d'Aulps	82
20c	Les cretes de Super Morzine	*	8	Vallee d'Aulps	82
21	Drouzin - Le Mont	*	8.5	Vallee d'Aulps	85
22	Les Lindarets	*	17	Vallee d'Aulps	87
27	Tour of La Pointe de Mirabel	*	8	Vallee Verte	102
28	Le Bachais	*	13	Vallee Verte	104
31	Samoens - Sixt	*	11	Vallee du Giffre	112
32	Plateau de Loex	*	12	Vallee du Giffre	114
37	La Chapelle Rambaud	*	16	Saleve	126
45	Chamonix (Bois du Bouchet)	*	15	Mont Blanc	150
3	Mont de Boisy	**	7	Bas Chablais	34
4	La Boucle des Allinges	**	17	Bas Chablais	36
5	Tete de Char (Targaillon)	**	14	Bas Chablais	38
6	Mont Forchat	**	15	Bas Chablais	40
10	Marin	**	14	Plateau du Gavot	53
11	From Bernex to Vinzier	**	20	Plateau du Gavot	56
12	The Gavot Plain 2	**	25	Plateau du Gavot	59
14	Lac des Plagnes	**	14	Val d'Abondance	66
15	Centfontaines	**	16	Val d'Abondance	68
23	The tour of Chery	**	11	Vallee d'Aulps	90
24	The Vallee d'Aulps	**	16	Vallee d'Aulps	92
25	Pointe de la Turche	**	17	Vallee d'Aulps	95
29	Petetoz	**	7	Vallee Verte	106
33	Lac de Gers	**	14	Vallee du Giffre	117
34	Sixt - Fer a Cheval	**	16	Vallee du Giffre	119

RATING
RIDE REFERENCE TABLE

NO	RIDE	RATING	KM	REGION	PAGE
35	Les Carroz	**	21	Vallee du Giffre	121
38	Le Saleve 1	**	8	Saleve	129
39	Le Saleve 2	**	12	Saleve	131
40	Groisy - Villy Le Bouveret	**	12	Saleve	133
41	Les Fretes	**	8	Bornes & Aravis	138
46	Le Bettex	**	11	Mont Blanc	152
7	Signal des Voirons	***	15	Bas Chablais	43
13	Pic des Memises	***	15	Plateau du Gavot	62
16	Champery	***	16	Val d'Abondance	71
17	The tour of Grincheux	***	19	Val d'Abondance	74
18	A tour of Mont Chauffe	***	19	Val d'Abondance	76
19	Chalets d'Autigny	***	25	Val d'Abondance	78
30	La Haute Pointe	***	15	Vallee Verte	108
36	A tour of Mole	***	11	Vallee du Giffre	123
42	Col des Annes	***	26	Bornes & Aravis	140
47	Col de Voza	***	22	Mont Blanc	155
48	Bionnassay	***	10	Mont Blanc	158
49	Chalet de Mayeres	***	10	Mont Blanc	160
50	Lac de Pormenaz	***	18	Mont Blanc	162
43	Lac de Lessy	****	13	Bornes & Aravis	143
44	Petit-Bornand	****	33	Bornes & Aravis	117
26	Saint-Jean d'Aulps	****	17	Vallee d'Aulps	97

DISTANCE
RIDE REFERENCE TABLE

NO	RIDE	RATING	KM	REGION	PAGE
20a	Les cretes de Super Morzine	*	3.5	Vallee d'Aulps	82
20b	Les cretes de Super Morzine	*	7	Vallee d'Aulps	82
3	Mont de Boisy	**	7	Bas Chablais	34
29	Petetoz	**	7	Vallee Verte	106
20c	Les cretes de Super Morzine	*	8	Vallee d'Aulps	82
27	Tour of La Pointe de Mirabel	*	8	Vallee Verte	102
38	Le Saleve 1	**	8	Saleve	129
41	Les Fretes	**	8	Bornes & Aravis	138
21	Drouzin - Le Mont	*	8.5	Vallee d'Aulps	85
1	Lake Geneva (Yvoire-Sciez)	*	9	Bas Chablais	29
48	Bionnassay	***	10	Mont Blanc	158
49	Chalet de Mayeres	***	10	Mont Blanc	160
2	Lake Geneva (Sciez-Allinges)	*	11	Bas Chablais	31
8	The Gavot Plain 1	*	11	Plateau du Gavot	48
31	Samoens - Sixt	*	11	Vallee du Giffre	112
23	The tour of Chery	**	11	Vallee d'Aulps	90
46	Le Bettex	**	11	Mont Blanc	152
36	A tour of Mole	***	11	Vallee du Giffre	123
32	Plateaux de Loex	*	12	Vallee du Giffre	114
39	Le Saleve 2	**	12	Saleve	131
40	Groisy - Villy Le Bouveret	**	12	Saleve	133
28	Le Bachais	*	13	Vallee Verte	104
43	Lac de Lessy	****	13	Bornes & Aravis	143
10	Marin	**	14	Plateau du Gavot	53
5	Tete de Char (Targaillon)	**	14	Bas Chablais	38
14	Lac des Plagnes	**	14	Val d'Abondance	66
33	Lac de Gers	**	14	Vallee du Giffre	117
45	Chamonix (Bois du Bouchet)	*	15	Mont Blanc	150
6	Mont Forchat	**	15	Bas Chablais	40
7	Signal des Voirons	***	15	Bas Chablais	43

DISTANCE
RIDE REFERENCE TABLE

NO	RIDE	RATING	KM	REGION	PAGE
13	Pic des Memises	***	15	Plateau du Gavot	62
30	La Haute Pointe	***	15	Vallee Verte	108
37	La Chapelle Rambaud	*	16	Saleve	126
15	Centfontaines	**	16	Val d'Abondance	68
24	The Vallee d'Aulps	**	16	Vallee d'Aulps	92
34	Sixt - Fer a Cheval	**	16	Vallee du Giffre	119
16	Champery	***	16	Val d'Abondance	71
22	Les Lindarets	*	17	Vallee d'Aulps	87
4	La Boucle des Allinges	**	17	Bas Chablais	36
25	Pointe de la Turche	**	17	Vallee d'Aulps	95
26	Saint-Jean d'Aulps	****	17	Vallee d'Aulps	97
9	Haut-Leman	*	18	Plateau du Gavot	50
50	Lac de Pormenaz	***	18	Mont Blanc	162
17	The tour of Grincheux	***	19	Val d'Abondance	74
18	A tour of Mont Chauffe	***	19	Val d'Abondance	76
11	From Bernex to Vinzier	**	20	Plateau du Gavot	56
35	Les Carroz	**	21	Vallee du Giffre	121
47	Col de Voza	***	22	Mont Blanc	121
12	The Gavot Plain 2	**	25	Plateau du Gavot	59
19	Chalets d'Autigny	***	25	Val d'Abondance	78
42	Col des Annes	***	26	Bornes & Aravis	140
44	Petit-Bornand	****	33	Bornes & Aravis	145

INFORMATION
RIDE REFERENCE TABLE

RIDE NO	NEAREST LOCATION FOR MOUNTAIN BIKE HIRE	LOCAL INFORMATION CENTRE	SKI LIFT AT START	SKI LIFT NEARBY
1	Douvaine or Sciez	50 94 10 55 / 50 72 64 57		
2	Sciez or Thonon	50 72 64 57 / 50 71 55 55		
3	Douvaine or Sciez	50 94 10 55 / 50 72 64 57		
4	Thonon	50 71 55 55		
5	Thonon	50 71 55 55		
6	Thonon	50 71 55 55		
7	Saxel	50 36 30 63		
8	Bernex	50 73 60 72		
9	Thollon	50 70 90 01		
10	Thonon	50 71 55 55		
11	Bernex	50 73 60 72		X
12	Bernex	50 73 60 72		
13	Thollon	50 70 90 01	X	
14	Abondance	50 73 02 90		X
15	Bernex or Abondance	50 73 60 72 / 50 73 02 90		X
16	Champery	025 79 11 41	X	X
17	Abondance, La Chapelle or Chatel	50 73 02 90		X
18	Abondance	50 73 02 90		X
19	Abondance	50 73 02 90		X
20	Morzine	50 79 03 45	X	X
21	Abondance	50 73 02 90		X
22	Morzine	50 79 03 45	X	X
23	Les Gets	50 75 80 80	X	X
24	Morzine	50 79 03 45		X
25	Les Gets	50 75 80 80	X	X

INFORMATION
RIDE REFERENCE TABLE

RIDE NO	NEAREST LOCATION FOR MOUNTAIN BIKE HIRE	LOCAL INFORMATION CENTRE	SKI LIFT AT START	SKI LIFT NEARBY
26	Morzine	50 79 03 45		X
27	Plaines Joux	50 35 91 83		X
28	Boege	50 39 11 28		
29	Habere Poche	50 39 54 46		
30	Taninges	50 75 80 80		
31	Samoens or Sixt	50 34 40 28 / 50 34 49 36		X
32	Les Gets	50 75 80 80		X
33	Sixt	50 34 49 36		
34	Samoens or Sixt	50 34 40 28 / 50 34 49 36		X
35	Les Carroz	50 90 00 04	X	X
36	Boneville	50 75 80 80		
37	Telepherique du Saleve	50 37 10 22		
38	Telepherique du Saleve	50 37 10 22	X	
39	Telepherique du Saleve	50 37 10 22		X
40	Telepherique du Saleve	50 37 10 22		
41	La Clusaz	50 02 60 92	X	X
42	Le Grand Bornand	50 02 20 33		X
43	St Jean de Sixt	50 02 70 14		
44	St Jean de Sixt	50 02 70 14		
45	Chamonix	50 53 00 24		X
46	St Gervais	50 78 22 43	X	
47	St Gervais	50 78 22 43	X	
48	St Gervais or Les Contamines	50 78 22 43 / 50 47 01 58	X	X
49	Sallanches	50 58 04 25		
50	Plateau d'Assy	50 58 80 52		

BAS-CHABLAIS

Lake Geneva is more than 70km long, 14km at its widest point and has 900 billion cubic metres of water. It is the largest lake in Western Europe so its importance to the climate and geography of Chablais in general and Bas Chablais in particular is obvious. The lake tempers the climate on the banks (and increases the rains in Haut Chablais). Enclosed by fairly low foothills, the plains which border the lake are suited to many forms of cultivation. The banks are dotted with numerous pleasure and fishing ports and with medieval towns and beaches which are an undeniable tourist attraction: Nernier, Yviore, Excenevex, Sciez and the domaine de Coudré, and of course Thonon, historic capital of Chablais.

Further beyond are the large arable fields, forests and then the vines which rise in tiers on the hills, and produce the Crépy and Marignan wines. The countryside inland is criss-crossed with little paths, swarming with villages and picturesque hamlets between which the countryside shows the importance of local agricultural activity. Then come the first wooded foothills with their long ridges which give marvellous views over Lake Geneva and over the nearby mountains to Mont Blanc in the distance.

Bas Chablais also has its rich and troubled history which goes back to the time of the first lake dwellings. Many different races have occupied this region - the Ligurians, the Allobrogians, and the Burgundians. They have left a good deal of evidence of their presence, of which the Châteaux Ripaille near Thonon is the most important.

1. THE SHORES OF LAKE GENEVA
From Yviore to Sciez

This is a pleasant ride between fields and forests over rolling terrain. Turning a bend, or from the top of a hill, you can often spot the nearby lake. The ride ends at Sciez which has a harbour and a beach.

Start	Yviore 390m	Duration	1 hour
Finish	Sciez	Rating	*
Distance	9km	Terrain	*
Climb	Negligible	Effort	*
Map	IGN 1:25000 3428 E		
Access	N5 from Thonon or Douvaine then D25 at Sciez, towards Excenevex.		

Route

Starting at the Town Hall, cycle up and over the D25. Go along a small road on the other side which runs between two camp sites. Carry on along a good path which comes out on to a main road, turn right to an oratory and then go on to the small village of Chevilly.

Cross the village and you will then come to a path which runs first through fields and then forests, and finally, as you turn a bend come to the D225. From there you climb up on the left for about 400m and then fork right and follow a hedge which will bring you to a forest path, running alongside a stream, which leads to Filly. Then go towards Sciez crossroads, keep on the left hand side of the road and then take the first left which leads to the Château of Coudrée. Turn right in front of the Château and you will come to Sciez harbour.

Additional information

It is possible to visit the Roman excavations near the Yvoire football pitch.

There is a beautiful sandy beach at Excenevex. For food lovers there is the luxurious hostellry at the Château of Coudrée.

1. THE SHORES OF LAKE GENEVA
From Yviore to Sciez

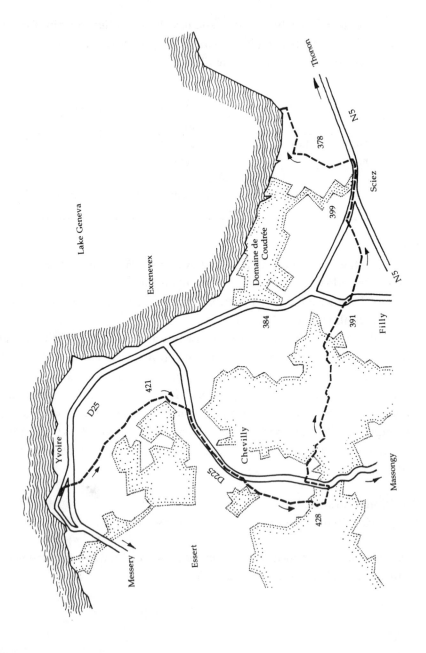

2. THE SHORES OF LAKE GENEVA
From Sciez to Allinges

Unlike the previous route, this ride leaves the Lake and goes further inland.
It ends at the very pretty village of Allinges at the base of the first hill just
above Thonon-les-Bains.

Start	Sciez 375m	Duration	1 - 2 hours
Finish	Allinges	Rating	*
Distance	11km	Terrain	**
Climb	200m	Effort	***
Map	IGN 1:25000 3428 ET		
Access	From Douvaine or Thonon via the N5.		

Route

From Sciez harbour take the N5 which leads to Sciez village and Ballaison-
Bons. Cross the village, go in front of a building development, and 400m
further on, fork left and go down a rocky and often slippery forest path to
Moulin Gorgux. Cross the old bridge which straddles the Foran stream. The
path continues on the opposite bank, leads to some buildings and runs down
on the right to another stretch of the stream. From there, it snakes through
the woods and comes out at the Choisy crossroads. This part is often very
damp so be extremely careful!

From Choisy (an equestrian centre) follow a small road for about 500m
until it turns right. Then take the path opposite which is by an electricity
pylon. A little further on cross a small road, and after the path has looped
round you will come out on to a main road. Follow the road to the right and
then to the left and cross the Redon bridge with its old windmill.

Take the D233 to the hamlet of Ronsuaz (you will see the crossroads and a
cross). Go in front of the wash-house and the fountain. Go downhill and
then climb up on the right towards the football pitch and Margencel. After
the church and the town hall, ride along for about 400m and just before a
crossroads with a figure of Christ, take the left hand path which crosses the
railway line. Follow the line and after a level crossing, you will come to
Mésinges.

Join the D903 and cross over to find a path which leads to Commelinges
and Allinges.

Additional information
You will find the protected site of 'Grand Marcis' in the communes of Margencal and Allinges. This site measures 23 hectares and is a perfect refuge for unusual flora and fauna. Once thought of as evil, marshes today are seen as useful and beneficial, bringing a rare diversity of vegetation and colour to the countryside whatever the season.

2.   THE SHORES OF LAKE GENEVA
From Sciez to Allinges

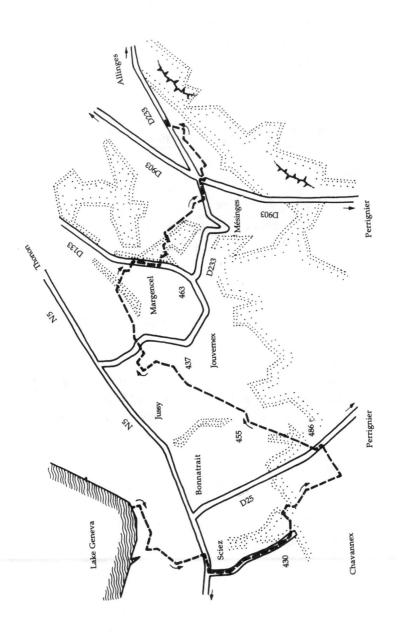

3. MONT DE BOISY
A Woodland Ride

Mont de Boisy overlooks Douvaine and Sciez above the west plain of the shores of Lake Geneva. On its sunny hillside the vines spread out facing the lake and the setting sun. This is the Crépy wine region (on the Douvaine heights), and the Marignan region (near Sciez).

Start	Les Crapons 604m	*Duration*	1 hour
Finish	Les Crapons	*Rating*	**
Distance	7km	*Terrain*	**
Climb	140m	*Effort*	**
Map	IGN 1:25000 3428 ET		
Access	From Thonon take the N5 to Sciez and then the D1 to Crapons.		

Route

Start from Crapons Nord (599m) and follow the end of the main road, and then a path which crosses fields and runs close to the Château of Boisy. Follow the right hand road for about 250m and then take the path on the right (road signs and a cross) which leads to the forest. Then continue along a beautiful bridle path which crosses the hill and ends at the Chapelle de Chavannex. From here it is easy to get back to Crapons by going through the houses of Varnaz.

Additional information

There is a lovely view of Lake Geneva from the Chapelle de Chavannex.

You can taste and buy a delicious bottle of Crépy wine (light and sparkling) from Robert Goy at Morcorens. The Château of Thérieres and Boisy are private property.

3. MONT DE BOISY
A Woodland Ride

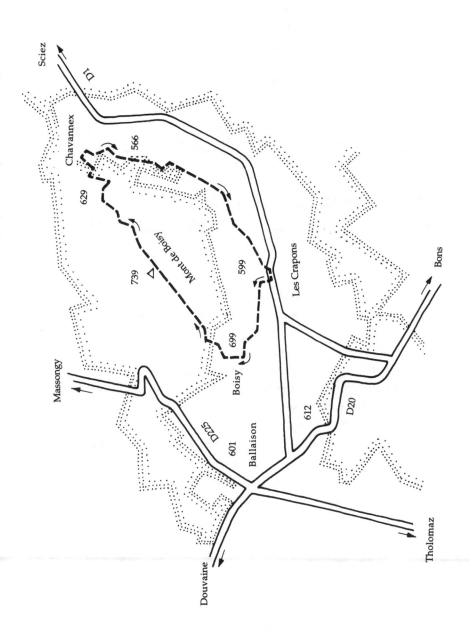

4. LA BOUCLE DES ALLINGES
Château and Hamlets

The Boucle des Allinges is a pretty, fairly easy ride which will enable you to go right round this little hill which overlooks Thonon. Unfortunately, little today remains of the two fortified castles whose watch towers used to survey the vast Léman plain.

Start	Perrignier 560m	Duration	2 hours
Finish	Perrignier	Rating	**
Distance	17km	Terrain	*
Climb	200m	Effort	**
Map	IGN 1:25000 3428 ET		
Access	From Thonon or Bons en Chablais via the D903.		

Route

From the centre of Perrignier climb up to the church which looks down over the village. Carry on towards Villard which is reached by following the Mas path on the right at 583m. Cross the village and before leaving it find a path which runs between the last houses and climbs up to the Maladière hill. For a time, the path becomes lost in the fields, but you can find it again just before the forest. Once out of the wood, fork right on to a path which leads to the houses at Chez Lagrange (695m) and then on to the small road which leads to the foot of the castles.

From there, first go down a section of main road, and then follow a good path to La Colombière (638m). From there, carry on down a path through fields to Bonnant. Here on the right, another path joins the small Villard road and the starting point of Perrignier.

Additional information

The Château of Allinges was once the home of François de Sales, a local historical figure. Do not miss the Allinges fresco in the castle which dates from the last third of the IV Century.

4. LA BOUCLE DES ALLINGES
Château and Hamlets

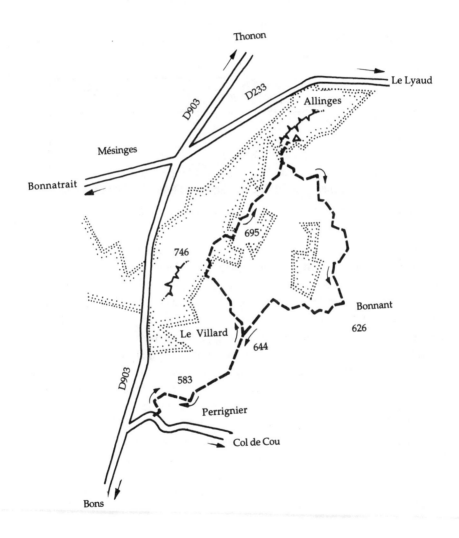

5. TÊTE DE CHAR-TARGAILLAN
From the Col de Saxel to the Col de Cou

This ride goes along the wooded backbone which leads from the col de Saxel to the col de Cou and follows the long Voirons ridge. The gradient is not a problem and the ride largely comprises of broad forest paths which are skiing pistes in winter. You will often find yourself following the walking route of the GR Balcon du Lêman.

Start	Col de Cou 1117m	Duration	1 - 2 hours
Finish	Col de Cou	Rating	**
Distance	14km	Terrain	**
Climb	300m	Effort	**
Map	IGN 1:25000 3429 ET		
Access	From La Vallée Vetre or Habère via the D12. Or from the Plaine du Chablais and Draillant via the D12.		

Route
On leaving the col go towards Habère Poche. About 100m further on, take the broad forest path which bears right into the woods, on the eastern side of the mountain. At a crossroads with signs, carry on up for a short stretch on a rather steep and unrideable path which reaches a spot height of 1188m. From here turn left, west, and cycle close to the summit of the Tête de Char (1249m) (not clearly marked). The path leads to a clearing from where you go down to Grange Billoud and then come up again under forest over to point 1212m.

From here, carry on along the ridge (marked 1275m) and you will then come back to the main road. Turn left towards Super Saxel and carry on to the crossroads (point 1098m) from where you climb up to the end of the road. From there, follow the wooded path which leads to Cabra and rejoins the ridge at point 1284m. Follow the ridge until you come back to the path and see the waymarks of Balcon du Léman just under point 1275m. Take the path followed on the outward stretch to point 1188m, just beyond the Tête de Char. Go down opposite on the western face of the summit at Targaillan and you will come back to the col de Cou.

Additional information
This trip is a fairly easy ride but includes some short steep stretches. Forest work (tree felling) can cause some obstacles.

5. TÊTE DE CHAR-TARGAILLAN
From the Col de Saxel to the Col de Cou

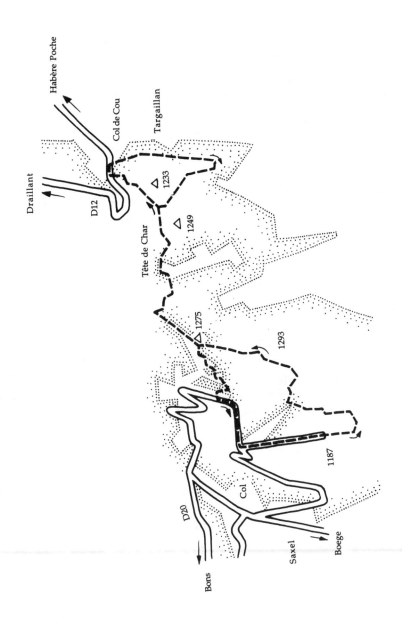

6. MONT FORCHAT
The Pilgrims' Path

Le Forchat is not a particularly high mountain (hardly more than 1500m) but it offers a lovely view which makes the climb very worthwhile.

It is a popular area for local walkers as the short climb makes for a pleasant family Sunday afternoon walk. So it is better to avoid Sundays in the high season, and at all time to be careful of the many walkers found in this area.

Start	Col de Feu 1120m	Duration	1 - 2 hours
Finish	Col de Feu	Rating	**
Distance	15km	Terrain	**
Climb	420m	Effort	**
Map	IGN 1:25000 3428 ET		
Access	From Lullin in the Vallée du Brevon on the D22, then the D35 which leads to the Col de Feu. From Perrignier Drailland or Orcier via the D35 up to the Col du Feu.		

Route

Start from the huge col de Feu car park, climbing the minor road which leads to Trés le Mont (1382m) and the end of the road. Carry on, passing the fencing, and forking quickly right to reach the forest. The fairly steep path climbs under the cover of trees but the surface is quite good. It leads into a pretty clearing (point 1504m) where you will find a small oratory made of wooden logs. From there, the path remains more or less level until the summit which you skirt around and come to the foot of the statue of St. François de Sales.

You descend a steep path where you will have to carry your bike for a short while until you reach a Col, unnamed on the IGN map at point 1513m. Go on in a northerly direction and you will come to Trés le Mont. You then go down on the minor road to the third bend (point 1310m) where you take the left hand (westward) path which leads to the alpine pastures of Trécout. From there, signs show the way back to the Col du Feu along a beautiful smooth wooded piste.

Variations

It is possible to do this ride the other way round, or to go down from the unnamed col to Habère Poche. It is also possible to reach the col des Moises from the coomb below Crêt Pujin, or even to reach the village of Draillant by way of Trécout and the D246.

Additional information

At Trés le Mont there is a simple pleasant alpine restaurant, 'Au Petit Savoyard'. Accommodation is available at Paul Maynet's Inn on the col de Feu.

6. MONT FORCHAT
The Pilgrims' Path

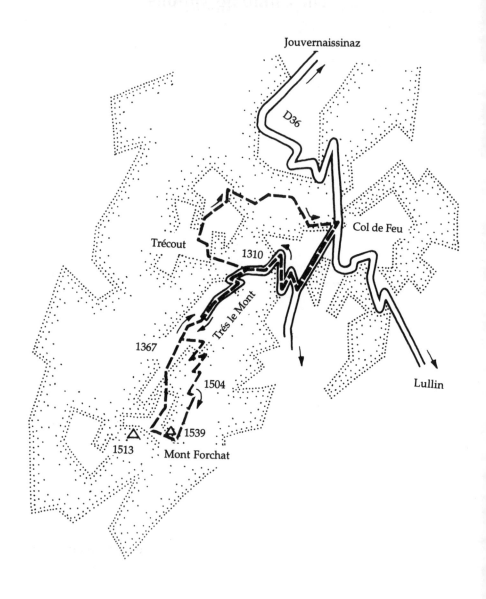

7. SIGNAL DES VOIRONS & THE POINTE DE BRANTAZ
The Climb up Voirons

The Voirons hill is on the southern most part of the foothills which demarcate the Léman plain. The large forests on its slopes shelter a large number of animals, and chamois and roe deer can often be seen. However, sighting a shy and secretive lynx would be much more unusual. The only problem with this ride is the sheer physical effort needed.

Start	Chemenoud 965m	Duration	2 - 4 hours
Finish	Chemenoud	Rating	***
Distance	15km	Terrain	**
Climb	520m	Effort	***
Map	IGN 1:25000 3429 ET		
Access	From Annemasse take the D206 towards Douvaine. At St Cergues turn right onto minor roads in the direction of Dombres. Continue on the twisting road to Chemenoud.		

Route

Start from the bend just before Chemenoud, marked on the map at spot height 965m. There, a wide mountain path follows the northern hillside and climbs up through the forest. It passes through Fieu and La Rive, forks right (point 1124m) and then skirts around the edge of the mountain and heads back to Moutonnière. From here it is best to take the Voirons road (coming from the col de Saxel) which passes in front of the Sisters of Bethlehem Convent. A path on the right leads up to the Voirons ridge and from there it is easy to reach the Pointe de Brantaz. You can also climb up to the Signal des Voirons (1480m) the highest point, by following the ridge on the right.

You go down along the GR Balcon du Léman which passes in front of the Chapelle de Notre Dame des Voirons and then heads back to Mautonnière. The rest of the return journey is the same as the outward in reverse.

Variations

From Mautonnière you can get back to the col de Saxel by following the waymarks of the GR road.

It is also possible to carry on southwards, beyond the Pointe de Brantaz and come down through Lucinges or Bonne sur Menoge.

Additional information

The convent area is a place for prayers and meditation, so try to be as inconspicuous as possible.

The view from Signal des Voirons is a just reward for all your efforts.

7. SIGNAL DES VOIRONS & THE POINTE
DE BRANTAZ
The Climb up Voirons

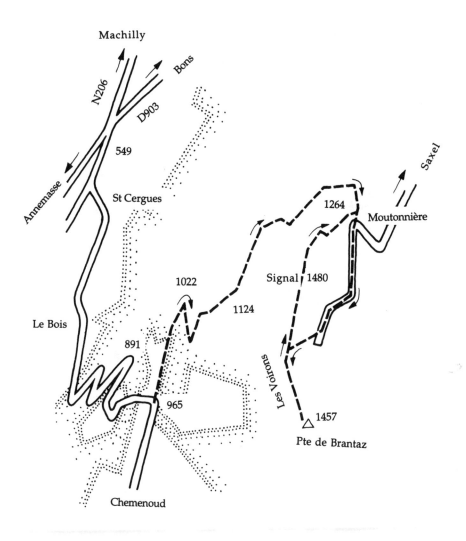

PLATEAU DE GAVOT

This eastern area of Chablais is one of the most popular tourist centres. It stretches from Evian in the west, on the shore of Lake Geneva, to the port and small town of St Gingolph on the Swiss frontier. The ancient town of Evian with its numerous historical dwellings (villa of the Lumière brothers, Château de Blonay) and its picturesque little alleyways is situated on the shore of the lake, and has captivated many a visitor. In the main street is the headquarters of the Evian mineral water producers, located in the former Hotel de Ville, where you can help yourself to their famous water from the spring at the entrance.

The pleasant and unspoilt countryside between the lake and mountains is a region of great contrasts and has a gentle sunny climate. At the upper end of the plain, set against a stunning mountain backdrop, is the golden triangle of mountain biking: St Paul, Bernex and Thollon-les-Mémises, which offers excellent opportunities for mountain bikers, be they beginners or experts! The Swiss border is only a mountain top away. But there is another side to the Gavot Plateau; old villages with well-to-do farms, fields and forest, fauna and flora, high mountain lakes, pure air, and not a sound to be heard except for the tinkling of cow-bells . . . The valleys lead south towards Abondance, covered in the next section.

8. THE GAVOT PLAIN 1
A Nature Snapshot

The Gavot Plain is covered with great stretches of woods and forests which surround old hamlets with working farms, whose ancient traditions still thrive. The area is unspoilt and well worth exploring.

Start	Vinzier 920m	*Duration*	1 -2 hours
Finish	Vinzier	*Rating*	*
Distance	11km	*Terrain*	*
Climb	Negligible	*Effort*	*
Map	IGN 1:25000 3428 ET, 3528 ET		
Access	From the D32 west of Bernex or the D21 from Larringes, to just outside Vinzier.		

Route
From the village drop down through Cambuse and the Granges farm to Divey (830m). From there cycle to the Mérou hamlet. Carry on through Chez les Giroud to Plantaz (719m). A path climbs alongside and leads to the Flon houses. Take this path which passes close to Sur les Crêts and you will soon come to the Champellant chapel (890m). Cycle through the hamlets of Nattay, Clouz and Théry (895m) to get back to Vinzier.

Variation
From the Champellant chapel it is easy to do a round trip through Chez Divoz, la Léchère and Larringes up to Chez Portay and then back to the chapel.

Additional information
From Champellant there is a lovely view over Mont Blanc.

Accomodation is available at the 'Ermitage des Clouz' gîte at Vinzier.

8. THE GAVOT PLAIN 1
A Nature Snapshot

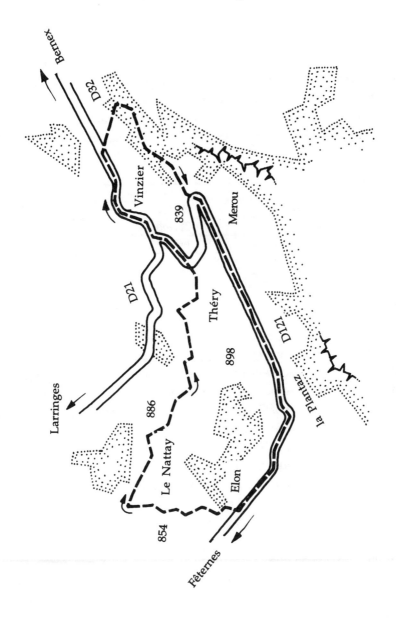

9. HAUT LÉMAN
Between Lake and Mountain

This region has villages and hamlets with melodious names - Neuvecelle, Maxilly, Lugrin, Tourronde. Here you will discover the joy of being in the countryside around Evian. Is it being so close to both lake and mountain which adds to the special atmosphere that you feel up here? Maybe, but take a look at the few remaining hardworking professional fishermen. Depending on the season, they catch fine and succulent perch, the famous Léman trout, the rare pike and the treasure of these waters, the noble 'fera' (a kind of still-water fish).

Start	Evian 375m	Duration	2 hours
Finish	Evian	Rating	*
Distance	18km	Terrain	*
Climb	Negligible	Effort	*
Map	IGN 1:25000 3528 ET		
Access	N5 from Thonon to quayside at Evian.		

Route

From the quays of Evian, take the D24 go through the Maraîche crossroads towards Montigny lake and cycle on to the villas of Trés le Cros (515m). Turn left on to the minor road which runs through the hamlet of Trives down to the houses of Prés de Bernex (443m). Near an oratory (a cross) a right hand path leads to the hamlet of Chez Busset. From there, go on to the old village of Véron with its fine small chapel (483m).

The path snakes down through the woods of Vallone and Rappe to the buildings at Combes, and comes out at Troubois. From there, go on to Lugrin by way of Raquaz and Rys. Carry on towards Chez Chatillon and Allaman and you will soon come to the shore of Lake Geneva at Blonay. The return leg to Evian runs through Torrat, Petite Rive and Grande Rive.

Variation

You can cycle along the N5 from Troubois to Meillerie, a quiet fishing village, immortalised by, among others, Jean-Jacques Rousseau, and the poet Lamartine.

We would recommend going back to Evian on one of the big CGN steamers (the timetable is available on the Evian landing stage).

Additional information

Accommodation is available at the Bois Ramé gîte at Neuvecelle (Verlagny).

One of the high points of this trip has to be the coastal cruise between Meillerie and Evian, if at all possible on 'Le Suisse', the flagship of the company. It is a boat with paddle wheels and its original machinery (1910) has two decks 10m long and 8.5m wide, and with 1400 horsepower, can carry up to 1500 passengers.

9. HAUT LÉMAN
Between Lake and Mountain

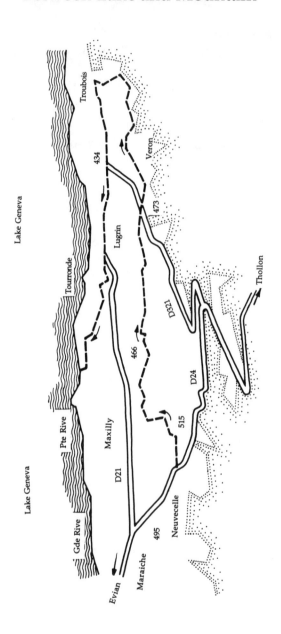

10. MARIN
The Heart of the Vineyards

Thanks to the climate, the Marin vineyard whilst very old, has been able to keep its particular character, and as the years pass, it has acquired a quality worthy of the great wines of Savoy. This Chablaision village is also known for cultivating its vines on 'crosiers'. This method of cultivation is carried out by means of a stripped chestnut tree planted in the ground and covered with five vine plants. Of Piemont origin, this method of grape production enables the vine to be less vulnerable to spring frosts which are harder at ground level.

Start	Marin 580m	Duration	1 - 2 hours
Finish	Marin	Rating	**
Distance	13.5km	Terrain	*
Climb	280m	Effort	**
Map	IGN 1:25000 3428 ET		
Access	D32 east from Thonon to Marin.		

Route
From the church car park, go down through Rouchaux to the sports complex. From there follow the wide path which runs through Fin de Publier and rejoins the D61. You will come to the edge of the hamlet of Moruel from where a path leads down to Avonnex. A small section of metalled road leads to Sussinges which you cross and go towards Chapelle and the D32, and then come to Vignes du Pont path on the left of a wide bend. Climb through the vines to the old farm of Cutle and the Chullien hamlet (625m). Follow the Léman path for a short distance which runs near the Gavot stables and leads back to Francalua and the bottom of the village at Champanges. Go down through Rimandon to get back to Marin.

Variations
From Champanges you can go down through Pierre des Gauloises and Bois Bernard to the hamlet of Avulligoz (550m) and finally come to Publier. Return to Marin by way of Moruel.

Additional information
It is well worth a stop at Gabriel and Pierre Floret's cellar to taste the dry and fruity Marin wine. We will leave the length of your stop up to you!

10. MARIN
The Heart of the Vineyards

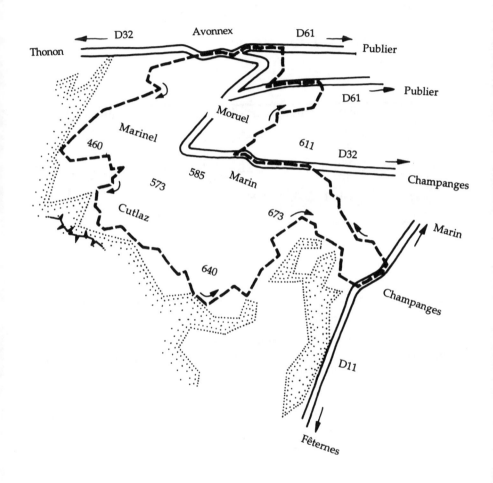

11. FROM BERNEX TO VINZIER
Dawdles in the Bernoland Countryside

A gentle bike ride is the best way to explore this part of the Chablaision countryside which still retains its pastoral quality. The contrasts will surprise you: looking towards Lake Geneva, you see green and gentle hills, on the other side you see harsh chalk rock faces!

Start	Bernex (church car park) 945m	Duration	2 hours
Finish	Bernex	Rating	**
Distance	20km	Terrain	**
Climb	415m	Effort	**
Map	IGN 1:25000 3528 ET		
Access	From St Paul on D52 or Vinzier on D152.		

Route

From the church car park go towards the chairlift departure point and then go on through Trossy and Charmet to the Malpasset barns. Climb up on the right to the Bécrêt chalets and then go down to Palud. From here, go along the Beunaz road through Trossy and Bernex. This circuit, waymarked in parts, will lead to the old hamlet of Roseires (935m) down a hill which needs some care!

Climb up to the lovely beauty spot of Gottetaz and follow the Saint-Paul road, leaving it on the left just before the Dent D'Oche garage. A pleasant path leads to the hamlet of Chez Bochet. From there, turn right for about 250m and then turn left into the forest, and you will come to the Pessay barn. Descend on the left, to a path which runs alongside the fields and leads to Chez Bochet.

To get back to Bernex you take the small country road of Plaine des Faverges, and then a wide path.

Variations

You can quite easily exclude the Roseires circuit (the downhill stretches could cause a beginner some problems.

Additional information

The fortified Bernex Church is worth a visit. There are wonderful view points all along this ride.

11. FROM BERNEX TO VINZIER
Dawdles in the Bernoland Countryside

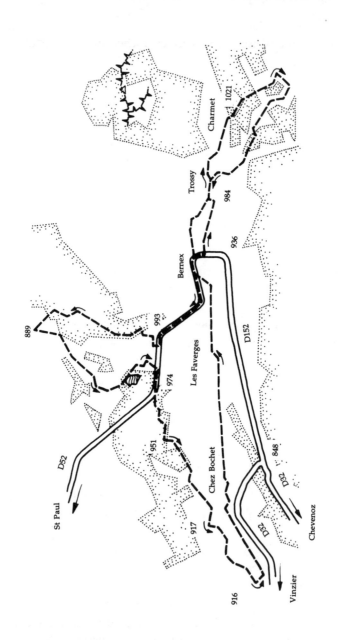

12. THE GAVOT PLAIN 2
Meanderings in Gavot

Good paths and small country roads, smelling of the fields and the forests, will enable you to exploit the rich diversity of this region.

Start	St Paul 820m	Duration	2 hours
Finish	St Paul	Rating	**
Distance	25km	Terrain	*
Climb	320m	Effort	**
Map	IGN 1:25000 3528 ET		
Access	Take D21 from Evian to D52 at St Paul.		

Route

From Saint Paul cycle to the hamlet at Coppy and the houses of Crêtes from where a path leads to the buildings of Chez Trincat. Bear right towards Le Bossons and Les Lacles (848m). The road runs in front of a cross and some buildings. On the left you will find the path which leads to Praubert (893) by way of Champs des Grives. After a stretch of road you will rejoin the path which climbs to the hamlet of La Jointe. Go towards Chez Gaillet and bear right on a wide path which crosses the Beunaz woods. The path continues through woodland to the houses of Champs du Bois (951m). From there, the sometimes rocky path snakes through the Fayet woods and comes out at the houses of Sous le Fayer (900m).

The road leads to Chez les Laurents (832m) through the hamlets of Chez Thiollay and Chez les Collomb. Fork left to come to a path which crosses fields to the forest of La Pastourelle and comes out at the village of Chez Crosson (800m) by way of Pesses à la Dame, and Perlatti. Cross the hamlet; go below the chapel and follow the path which leads to the stronghold at Larringes (798m). Carry on to the houses of Chez Desbois and take a left hand path which leads to the village of Champanges through Les Viots (710m) and La Combe.

From the village, the Saint-Martin road leads to the Maravant torrent (by the Croix Diochat). On the left after the bridge there is an old country track which leads to the buildings at Vers les Granges (891m) through Beule, Pré,

Plagnet, and Les Bois du Ban. To get back to Saint Paul, cycle in the direction of Maravant, la Fouly, les Ingers, and Vers de Four.

Additional information

From Champanges you can go down to the hamlet of Darbon (680m) to see the last oil crusher left in the region.

12.   THE GAVOT PLAIN 2
Meanderings in Gavot

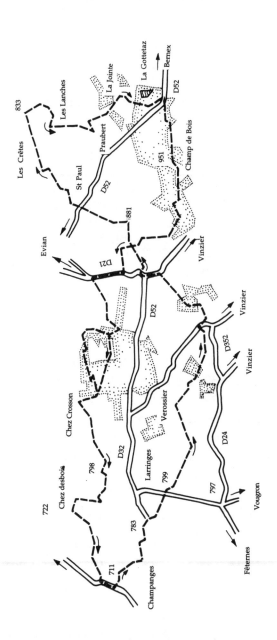

13. PIC DES MÉMISES
Le Balcon du Léman

A wonderful view awaits mountain lovers from this summit; straight ahead are the valleys and hills of the Jura, over the lake to the right is Switzerland and the Fribourg mountains and then the Swiss Alps. Then come the impressive 4000m mountains of Valois, with their permanent ice and finally the Chablaision summits, and all this is set off by the blue waters of lake Geneva.

Start	Thollon 1014m	*Duration*	3 hours
Finish	Thollon	*Rating*	***
Distance	15km	*Terrain*	***
Climb	200m	*Effort*	**
Map	IGN 1:25000 3528 ET		
Access	D24 from Evian to ski lift station at Thollon.		

Route

From the skiing resort of Thollon, take the cable car which rises to the top of the skiing pistes (1598m). There is no problem with taking a bike. You will come to the chalets of Mémises (1636m) by following a piste across alpine fields. Then find the broad path (somewhat steep) which leaves from the right of the Frasse chairlift and heads down to the col de Corniens (1462m). Then carry on to the Cornien Chalets (1393m) tucked away in their green surroundings. The descent starts down a lovely forest piste (what a joy to be on a bike!) and ends below the Chez Jacquier houses (Lejoux hamlet). A small section of metalled road takes you to the path which ends at the Reboux ruins (860m). The path widens and comes to the hamlet of Mercuant (962m) through the Pesse Vacle woods, and from there a local road leads on to Leucel. From there you go towards Nouy, Chez les Aires, and finally back to Thollon.

Additional information

Drinking water is available at the Corniens Chalets. Try to do this ride at the beginning of Autumn when the atmosphere and the colours are almost unreal. The surface is sometimes rather muddy, but this is nothing compared to the pleasure of the downhill sectors.

13. PIC DES MÉMISES
Le Balcon du Léman

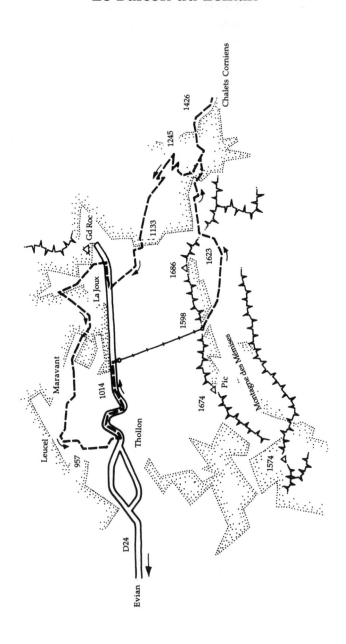

VAL D'ABONDANCE

The Val d'Abondance is without doubt one of the richest and most beautiful regions of Haute-Savoie. Thanks to a temperate climate, influenced largely by Lake Geneva, the valley has considerable forest cover (spruces, fir trees and beeches), as well as rich alpine fields where the traditional Abondance cheese is still made, which is a main ingredient of 'Barthoud', a typical Chablaisian speciality.

You can easily imagine the power and influence of this area during the time of the old Duchy of Savoy, as its history has been carefully preserved. The geographical isolation of the valley has enabled it to retain its traditional character. The communes of this valley (Chévenoz, Vacheresse, Bonnevaux, Abondance, la Chapelle and Châtel) offer hospitality, relaxation and nature. Winter sports are the main activity further up the valley, with La Chapelle d'Abondance and Châtel, close to the Swiss frontier at Pas de Morgins, being main centres and holiday villages.

This is a fantastic area for mountain biking, with wonderful excursions, paths and tracks leading through picturesque hamlets and alpine fields to mountain summits where the air is pure and exhilarating and there are spectacular views.

14. LAC DES PLAGNES
Climbing through Alpine Fields

The pretty little lake of Plagnes, embedded at the foot of the mountain, and delicately positioned among the blues and greens of the forest, is a meeting place for trout fishermen. The paths which lead from its banks allow the local herds to reach the alpine pastures at Lenlevay and Lens, where for some alpine dwellers, the traditions of old can be rediscovered.

Start	Lac des Plagnes 1191m	Duration	2 hours
Finish	Lac des Plagnes	Rating	**
Distance	14km	Terrain	*
Climb	540m	Effort	**
Map	IGN 1:25000 3528 ET		
Access	From Abondance take the telecabine route to the lake.		

Route
From the lake follow the wide piste which climbs to the chalets of Lens (1547m) and goes on to join the GR5 which in turn leads to the alpine pastures of Lenlevay (1733m). Go down to the chalets at Jouly and then to Bailly (1540m) and you will then come to the chapel of St. Théodule. From there you can easily retrace your steps to the starting point by following the local road.

Additional information
Water is available at the chalets of Lens and Lenlevay. There is a lovely view across the surrounding summits. Some alpine dwellers offer visits to see the traditional cheese making of Abondance. Do not hesitate to ask the owners .

14. LAC DES PLAGNES
Climbing through Alpine Fields

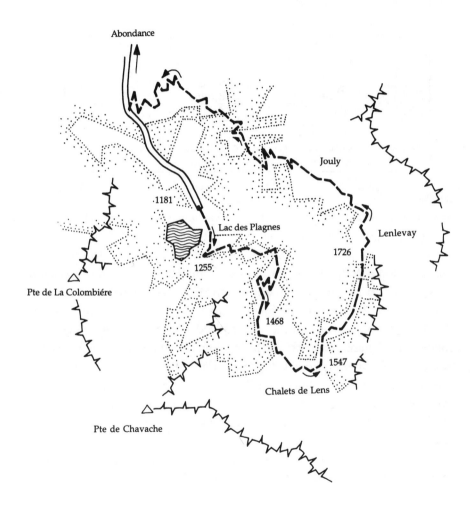

15. CENTFONTAINES
A Ride between Dranse and the Mountains

This route crosses magnificent countryside and will allow you to discover the full potential of your mountain bike.

Start	Gîte - 810m Centfontaines	Duration	2 hours
Finish	Centfontaines	Rating	**
Distance	16km	Terrain	**
Climb	200m	Effort	**
Map	IGN 1:25000 3528 ET		
Access	Gîte is on D22, between Vacheresse and Bonnevaux.		

Route
From the gîte, cycle along to the village of Vacheresse and come to the hamlet of Villard which you cross by means of a little road on the right. Continue towards La Revenette and follow the Bise road until you come to a chalet on the left hand side (point 940m). Leave the metalled road and go down a grassy track on the right which leads to an abandoned chalet and meets up with a mountain stream lower down (l'Eau Noire). The path (which is often flooded with water early in the season) leads to La Revenette where you follow the left hand road after the little bridge. Then there is a steep descent and on the left after a second bridge you climb a forest path which ends (on the right) at the Centfontaines road. The road goes down and on the left at an intersection, take the local path which runs alongside the Fiogère cliff. 500m after passing a house on the right go down a wide path which narrows down and comes out at the sawmill (take care).

From here follow the forest piste of L'Epine on the right near the old school to reach the village of Bonnevaux. Go in front of the water tower and continue along a track across the fields until you come to a steep acrobatic descent which leads to the houses of Chez Morard. Cycle on to Ecotex and then go down on the right to the Pont de la Cour. Climb back up to Fontany and then Vacheresse, and go back towards Centfontaines, the starting point.

Variation

It is possible to start below the Col du Corbier on the Muret road which joins the Epine piste by way of Les Rez. To get back to your car you will have to climb the col du Corbier road.

Additional information

It is possible to park at the Centfontaines gîte but check first. Food and accommodation are also available.

15. CENTFONTAINES
A Ride between Dranse and the Mountains

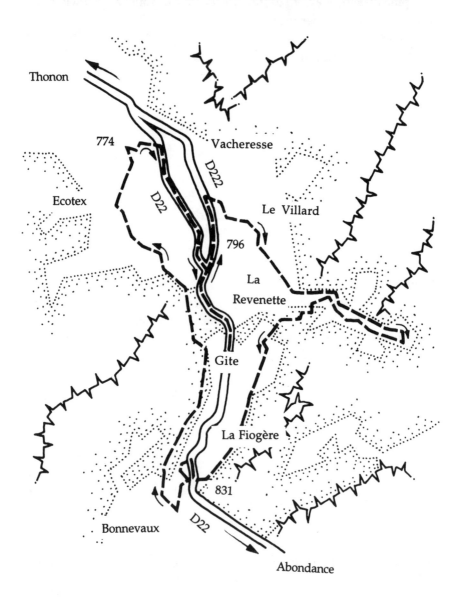

16. CHAMPÉRY
Towards the col de Cou

There are numerous points of interest on this route, two of which are the wonderful view over the massif of the Dents du Midi, the seven 'teeth', the highest of which, la Haute-Cime, reaches 3257m in height, and the small town of Champéry which has remained unspoilt.

Start	Champery - Switzerland	Duration	3 hours
Finish	Champery	Rating	***
Distance	16km	Terrain	**
Climb	290m	Effort	**
Map	CNS 1:25000 Val d'Illiez 1034		
Access	Enter Switzerland through Châtel and Pas de Morgins, through Val d'Illiez to Champery.		

Route

Go towards the departure station for the Planachaux télépherique which is right next to the Champéry sports complex (follow the tracks). The high-tec Planachaux télépherique enables you to reach the real starting point at 1963m in a few minutes. Take the four wheel drive road for about 1km, then bear right on a path which follows the western ridge. Go past the Chavanette chairlift (1840m) and go towards the Pointe de Ripaille (1927m) and carry on to the building of Lapisa (1788m).

From there go down for a short way to the fields of Ripaille (1753m) and then on to the chalet of La Pierre (1675m) and you will then reach the pastures of Le Poyat (1640m). The col de Cou, crossing point between the valley of the Manche and Haute-Savoie is not very far for those who are interested. However, it will take a bit of effort!

The descent starts towards Creuses. The path snakes through woods and fields following the bed of the Vièze river and rejoins the four wheel drive road which, after passing through la Haute Revène and the Parses forest ends at the top of the village of Champéry, the final stop on this difficult journey.

Variation
If you wish to avoid the télépherique the journey can be done in reverse.

Additional information
The little train which climbs from Monthey is one of the best examples of narrow gauge railways, of which the Swiss are such experts.

Jean-Denis Perrin, a loyal friend, fashions the famous bronze clocks of Champéry from antique moulds. Pay him a visit!

You can sample tomato fondue in the Val d'Illiez. Another speciality of this valley.

16. CHAMPÉRY
Towards the col de Cou

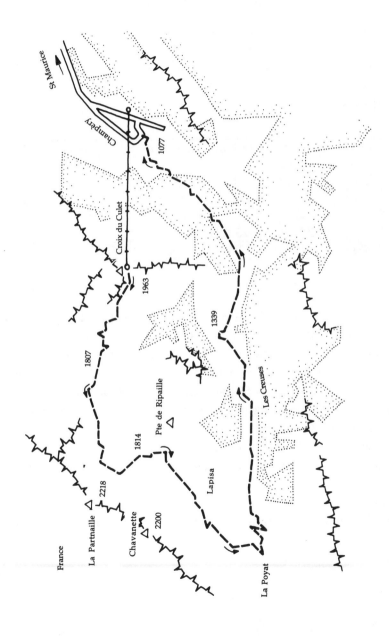

17. THE TOUR OF GRINCHEUX
A Circuit from the col de Bassachaux

This route already has a reputation. It must be one of the most difficult rides purely because of the number of ups and downs. Never mind, you are in a green setting, where you can pause for a snack in the shade of an old alpine chalet, and share your sense of wonderment with a small collection of friends. This expedition is one of the classics of the area.

Start	Col de Bassachaux 1778m	Duration	3 - 4 hours
Finish	Col de Bassachaux	Rating	***
Distance	19km	Terrain	***
Climb	330m	Effort	***
Map	IGN 1:25000 3528 ET		
Access	D226 from Châtel then D228 to the Col.		

Route

From the col de Bassachaux car park follow the road for about 200m and bear left on to a path which leads down to the chalets of Grands Plans. From there go down to the alpine chalets of Lenlevay on the GR5 and continue below the Coicon ridge to the chalets of Etrye (1694m). The path, which is very rocky in places, leads to the chalet of Cornillon and carries on to Boudimes. Depending on the season, it is possible to spot large numbers of chamois all along this route.

The long downhill sector which leads to the Ville de Nant (1040m) is as much a treat for the beginner mountain biker as for the greatest champion.

Variation

It is possible to go down from the chalets of Etrye to the chalets of Ertre.

Additional information

Water is available at the chalets of Lenlevay, Etyre and Boudimes. You will come out in the protected beauty spot at Mont de Grange so pay it due respect!

17. THE TOUR OF GRINCHEUX
A Circuit from the col de Bassachaux

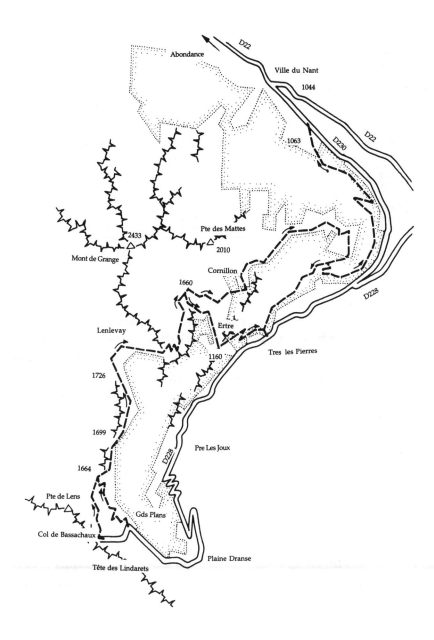

18. A TOUR OF MONT CHAUFFÉ
A Unique Experience

Le Mont Chauffé, with its huge vertical rock faces (more than 400m), is recognisable from afar wherever you are, as it rises up like an immense citadel right in the middle of the valley. Circling it on a mountain bike you will become aware of its characteristics.

Start	Abondance 920m	Duration	3 - 4 hours
Finish	Abondance	Rating	***
Distance	19km	Terrain	***
Climb	1050m	Effort	**
Map	IGN 1:25000 3528 ET		
Access	Off D22 at Abondance (same as route 19).		

Route

On leaving Abondance, cycle to the hamlet of Mont (1160m) and the col de la Plagne du Mont (1546m). From here go down to the Ubine chalets (1485m) and you will reach the col of the same name (1694m). From there, a section of road (rather tricky as it is very steep), leads to the 'off-road' vehicle track on the piste which in turn leads to the Mens chalets, and continues on to the Chevenne chalets (1248m). A small road leads to the Chapelle d'Abondance which you go through to reach the picturesque village of Abondance.

Variation

It is possible to go by way of La Batelle instead of crossing the village of La Chapelle d'Abondance.

Additional information

The northern face of Mont Chauffé is one of the best spots for rock climbing in Chablais. A part of this route runs through the protected beauty spot of Cornettes des Bise so respect the country code.

18. A TOUR OF MONT CHAUFFÉ
A Unique Experience

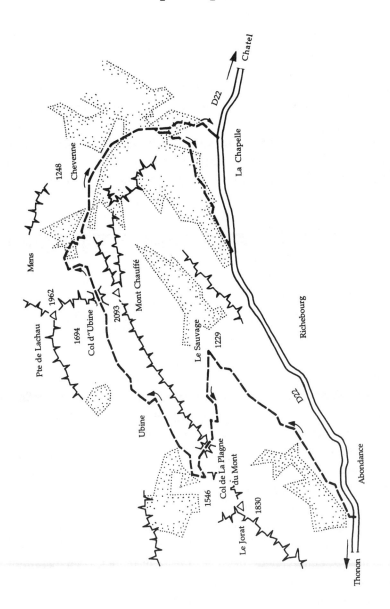

19. CHALETS D'AUTIGNY
A Mountain Worth Discovering

La Pointe d'Autigny could be compared to a futuristic fortress, protecting, with all its might, access to the Bise valley, and entry to the Plaine d'Abondance. Unfortunately, the western side from the chalets of Autigny onwards offers very little pleasure to any mountain lover: giant electricity pylons supporting high tension cables have taken over the area, totally ruining it with their ugliness.

When will people realise the value of the alpine countryside for our economic and cultural future? Let us not forget that one of the primary motivations of the potential tourist is also the rich beauty of our natural heritage.

Start	Abondance 920m	Duration	3 - 4 hours
Finish	Abondance	Rating	***
Distance	25km	Terrain	***
Climb	1050m	Effort	**
Map	IGN 1:25000 3528 ET		
Access	Off D22 at Abondance (same as route 18).		

Route

From Abondance take the road which leads to the Mont hamlet (1160m) from where a wide country path climbs through sparse woodland to the Sauvage building and leads to the col de la Plagne du Mont (1546m). From the col you can see the chalets of Autigny which are soon reached (1590m). You just have to stop here: the summit with its three crosses, about 30 minutes away on foot, offers marvellous views.

Go down from the Autigny chalets to the col de la Plagne du Mont, and then by way of an at times wooded path you will come to the pastures and chalets of Ubine (1485m). From here, follow the road which leads down to the houses of La Revenette passing in front of the Paraz chapel (built in a craggy rock as a precaution).

A section of main road then leads to Bonnevaux. You could also take the local path which follows the Fiogère Cliff. From there, take the local road to the old buildings of Plan Drouzin, and then on to the hamlets of Tronchet and Les Granges from where it is easy to get back to Abondance.

Additional information
Beautiful viewpoints throughout this trip. Water is available at the chalets of Autigny and at Ubine.

19. CHALETS D'AUTIGNY
A Mountain Worth Discovering

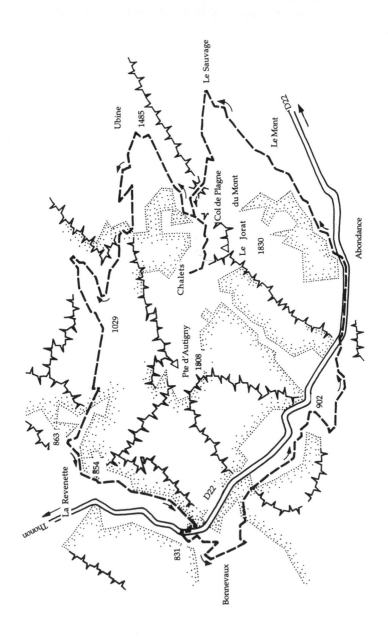

VALLÉE D'AULPS - HAUT-CHABLAIS

As you will gather from its name, this area has the highest peaks with Les Hauts Forts at 2464m being the highest. The main valley is the Vallée d'Aulps. The Dranse de Morzine river flows through it and joins the Dranse d'Abondance and the Brevon de Bellevaux downstream. Together these waters form the Dranse which flows into Lake Geneva.

The Vallée d'Aulps, like the Vallée d'Abondance, begins at this confluence in Bioge, but it is really only at Jotty that it really gets going. From there villages and hamlets rise up on both sides of the valley. Overlooked by the high summits the countryside is covered with forests and alpine pastures. These fields have mainly been created by clearances (as the village names of Essert la Pierre and Essert Roman reveal) and the work was largely done by monks. The abbey ruins at St Jean d'Aulps (destroyed during the French Revolution) give evidence of the monastic influence of the Middle Ages.

Today, active farming is still very evident in the Vallée d'Aulps despite the fact that the ski slopes of Morzine and Avoriaz have acquired international renown. Happily tourism has not really spoiled this area which cannot always be said elsewhere. Les Gets is near Morzine and even though it is in the Faucigny region it seemed more logical to include the routes in this section.

Le Haut-Chablais is a wonderful green pastoral area most definitely picture-postcard Haute-Savoie.

20. LES CRÊTES DE SUPER MORZINE
To the Worthless Mountain

This route crosses the Super Morzine ridges from the top of the Zore chairlift. You can go back by way of the Serrausaix mountain, or by the coombs to the Super Morzine télécabine. You can also chose to go down and back to the centre of Morzine by way of Les Déchères. Whatever route you choose the technical and physical difficulties are negligible.

Start	Zore chairlift 1760m	Duration	1 - 2 hours
Finish	Morzine	Rating	*
Distance	3.5, 7, 8km	Terrain	*
Climb	Negligible	Effort	*
Map	IGN 1:25000 3530 ET		
Access	From Thonon or Les Gets on D902.		

Route

From the centre of Morzine, near the sports centre by the river, take the Super Morzine télécabine and then the Zore chairlift. From there follow the wide piste eastwards towards Avoriaz. You will quickly reach the col de Serrausaix (1756m) and then the col de Joux Verte at 1760m.

From here there are three choice:

20a Follow the Avoriaz road for about 700m before going down on the right through the fields of Avoriaz mountain towards point 1664m. Continue on in the forest in the Creux de le Joux and then go by point 1634, keeping close to the road, before joining it a little further on; follow it to the Zore houses and the arrival point of the télécabine.

20b Go down the Joux Verte road to Sur l'Envers and then take the piste which leads off on the left towards Joux Verte, and cross the coombs which overlook Montriond lake. Go through point 1733m before crossing the col de la Croix des Combes at 1637m. Go down on the left and you will come to the Zore houses. Bear right towards the houses of Zore de Montriond (1499m) and then left to the Super Morzine télécabine.

20c If you prefer to go down to Morzine on your bike, you should go to le maison Neuve and then l'Elé from the Zore de Montriond houses. Cross the Montriond roads and go towards the village for about 100m, and then go down to the Deréches bridge. Return to Morzine by passing the swimming pool and the sports complex and following the Dranse riverbank of your choice.

Additional information

A lovely open view from the Super Morzine ridges. The coombs shelter numerous chamois.

20. LES CRÊTES DE SUPER MORZINE
To the Worthless Mountain

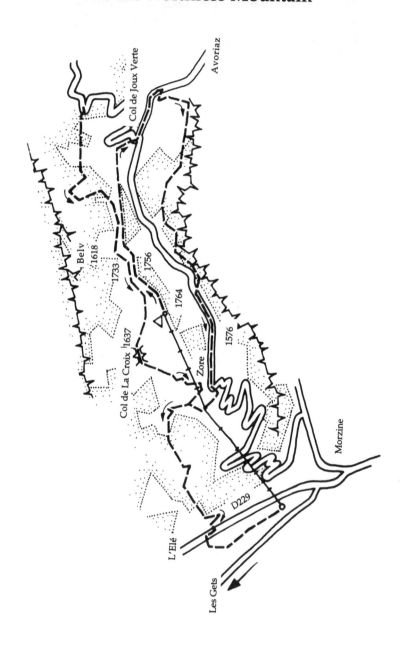

21. DROUZIN LE MONT
Between the Val d'Abondance and the Val d'Aulps

A good road enables you to climb easily to the alpine chalets of Drouzin from the col du Corbier, the old crossing point between the valleys of Aulps and Abondance. As you climb you will have a glorious view over numerous summits: Mont Chauffé, Cornettes de Bise, Mont Ouzon, Mont Billiat and others.

Start	Col du Corbier 1237m	Duration	1 hour
Finish	Col du Corbier	Rating	*
Distance	8.5km	Terrain	*
Climb	270m	Effort	*
Map	IGN 1:25000 3528 ET		
Access	Between Biot and Bonnevaux on D32.		

Route
From the col climb up a good piste which runs alongside a tennis court. At the edge of the forest follow a right hand piste which climbs to the Praux chalets (1356m). Signs show the piste to take: the one that leads to the col de Droline (1467m) and then to the chalets of Drouzin (1505m) and the end of this climb.

Go down towards the top of the chalets and you will find a barely visible track which leads to the col de Droline, and from there you can dash down the piste back to the starting point.

Variation
From Drouzin it is possible to continue on to the chalets of Thex and then you will come to Le Biot.

Additional information
Accommodation and food are available in the warm and rustic gîte at Bonnevaux.

Water replenishment is possible from the drinking trough at Drouzin. There is a beautiful view all the way up to Col de Droline.

21. DROUZIN LE MONT
Between the Val d'Abondance and the Val d'Aulps

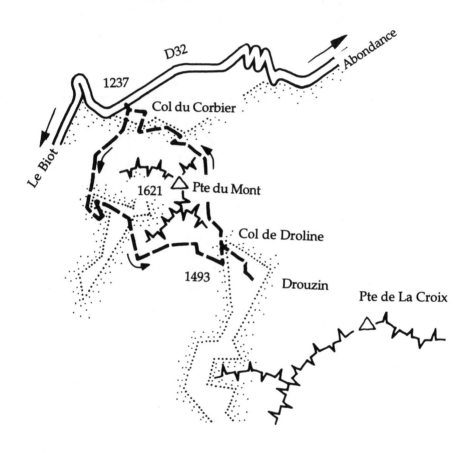

22. LES LINDARETS
The Downhill Option

This route is mainly described for its downhill sectors which lead off from the ridges of Super Morzine, but you will also see the 'goat' village of Lindaret and the banks of lake Montriond.

Start	Zore chairlift 1760m	Duration	2 - 3 hours
Finish	Morzine	Rating	*
Distance	17km	Terrain	**
Climb	860m of descent	Effort	*
Map	IGN 1:25000 3530 ET		
Access	From Thonon or Les Gets on D902.		

Route

Take the Super Morzine télécabine from the middle of the resort and then the Zore chairlift. From there follow the broad piste which leads to Avoriaz and the col de Serrausaiz at 1756m. Go down on the left towards the viewpoint and 1733m. Turn right towards Joux Verte and Sur l'Envers and come to the col de la Joux Verte road. Follow it down for about 100m, cross the clearing and carry on, after a short climb into the side of the forest, go under the ski lifts of La Lécherette, and you will come to Brocheau. Then go down into the valley to reach Les Lindarets. Follow the road or the skiing pistes to Ardent.

From here go towards the waterfall and then on to Albertans. Follow the path which leads to the end of the lake, and follow the lake round on the left until you come to the pleasure beach. Carry on down the forest path until it joins to the road. Climb up, slightly on the right until you come to the lake road, 'Par le Crêt'. Immediately on the left of the road join a path which follows the left bank of the Dranse de Montriond, and then take the road which leads to the Glière bridge. Cross the bridge and then take the D229 towards the campsite and climb the right hand bank of the Dranse, through Les Dérèches to the Morzine sports complex.

Additional information

The goat village at Lindarets is very touristy but quite fun! In the upper rock faces below the coombs which overlook Montriond lake you will still find old slate quarries which were once one of the riches of the area.

The Ardent waterfall is impressive.

22. LES LINDARETS
The Downhill Option

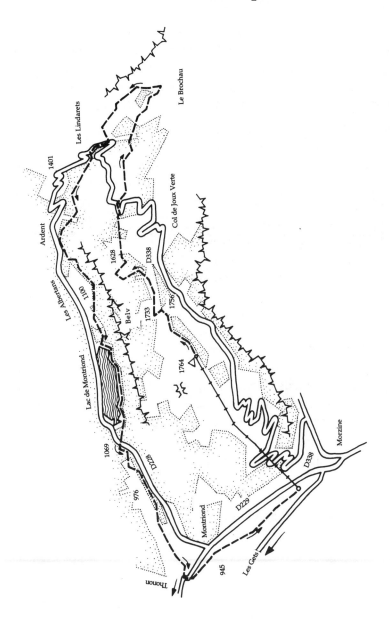

23. THE TOUR OF CHERY
Around the Large Bosses

Le Chéry is the Les Gets mountain and we are certainly talking large bosses; bosses which envelope the summit (1826m) with their soft, broad shape. Mont Chéry appears even more welcoming because of the contrast with the soaring ridges of the Roc D'Enfer. You can cycle round Mony Chéry by starting from Mont Caly, or the top of the télécabinee, or from the col de l'Encrenaz, but the route below starts from Lassare.

Start	Lassare 1337m	Duration	1 -2 hours
Finish	Lassare	Rating	**
Distance	11km	Terrain	**
Climb	Negligible	Effort	*
Map	IGN 1:25000 3528 ET		
Access	Outside Les Gets on D902, take minor road to Mont Chery telcabine station and Lassare.		

Route

From Lassare a good wooded road goes towards the north face of the mountain. The road follows the side of the mountain, rising very little, until it approaches the col de L'Encrenaz at 1433m. From there carry on climbing gently and go under the last ski lift and continue along the forest path which leads to point 1493m before reaching Mont Caly. To get back to Lassare cycle by way of Les Fontanettes, Les Moraines, the arrival station of the télécabine and finally through the Lassare pastures.

Additional information

The skiing village of Les Gets is home to the museum of mechanical music, especially worth visiting for its huge organ.

23. THE TOUR OF CHERY
Around the Large Bosses

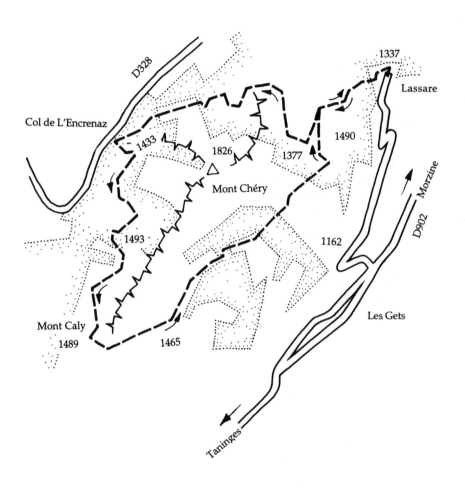

24. MEANDERINGS IN THE VALLÉE D'AULPS
Landmarks of History

This route runs along old paths which are somewhat underused today. With its great height, Mont Billiat towers over the old village of Baume, which was, together with his hamlet of Chez le Geydets, once the fiefs of Uncle Jack, a Savoyard hero who committed numerous brave acts against the French revolutionary troops. Then you come to the Sistercian Monastery of Aulps built in the XI Century and of which only ruins remain. Quite apart from spreading the faith, the monks contributed much to the development of the high alpine villages by their important work in the fields of agriculture, teaching and medicine.

Start	La Baume 720m	Duration	2 hours
Finish	La Baume	Rating	**
Distance	16km	Terrain	**
Climb	300m	Effort	**
Map	IGN 1:25000 3528 ET		
Access	From Thonon, south on D902 to Le Jotty then right onto D232 to La Baume.		

Route

From the church car park climb towards the chalets of La Goutreuse (874m) along the local road. The slope will bend round and steadily reach the small hamlet of Urine. After the last houses, a wide path on the right leads through fields and forests to the hamlet of Sey at Seytroux. Go on to the town hall and pass the buildings at Combes and join the D193. After the bridge this road will climb up to the hamlet of Bas-Thex (802m) and meander on to the monastery and Saint Jean d'Aulps.

We would recommend retracing your steps to Bas-Thex (802m). From here a good path winds through the forest and leads to the village of Biot. From the town hall, follow a path which leads down to the hamlet of Coudre. Cross the Couvaloup bridge (696m) and continue on to the houses of Chez les Geydets, and Promerat, and then return to Baume.

Additional information

Refreshment are available on many parts of this route. Do go and visit Fëlix at Le Baume, for his cheeses, his local charcuterie, and of course for his hospitality!

24. MEANDERINGS IN THE VALLEÉ D'AULPS
Landmarks of History

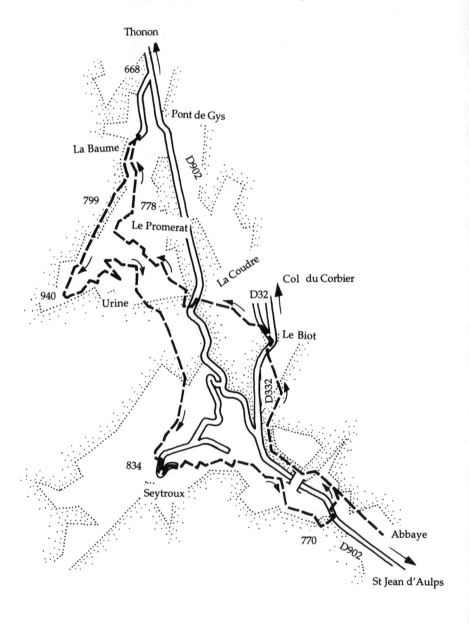

25. POINTE DE LA TURCHE
The Skiing Area of Gets

The Chavannes side of Les Gets is used for skiing but it is also quite suitable for mountain biking. There are superb views from the ridges.

Start	Les Chavannes 1484m	Duration	2 hours
Finish	Les Chavannes	Rating	**
Distance	17km	Terrain	*
Climb	260m	Effort	**
Map	IGN 1:25000 3530 ET		
Access	To Les Gets on D902. Right past church on access road to Chavannes.		

Route

Follow the route up to Chavannes, signposted from the village centre, along the path which runs under a ski lift and heads towards the equestrian centre. Carry on along this piste which stays fairly level until going down to the bottom of several ski lifts at point 1404m.

Climb this piste to 1429m and then turn to the west to the arrival station of the Turche ski lift at 1516m (a cross at point 1607m) and le Turche Noire (1665m).

Then go down to Lairon and return across the plains of bilberries and rhododendrons, passing under the chairlifts of Ranfolly and La Mouille aux Chats, and the ski lift of Plan des Nauchets.

Additional information

The numerous ski lifts and demarcated pistes do not exactly add to the beauty of the countryside! Should not the beauty of the Alps be a part of our cultural heritage which we should be keen to preserve?

25. POINTE DE LA TURCHE
The Skiing Area of Gets

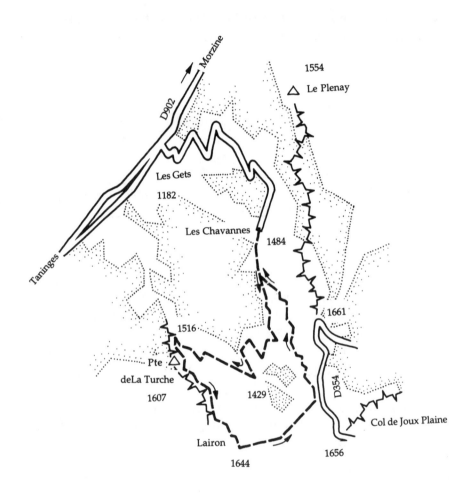

1554
Le Plenay

Morzine

D902

Les Gets
1182

Les Chavannes
1484

Taninges

1661

1516

Pte
deLa Turche
1607

1429

D354

Col de Joux Plaine

Lairon
1644

1656

26. SAINT JEAN D'AULPS
At the Foot of Roc d'Enfer

This wonderful expedition has not yet won the reputation it deserves. Perhaps it is a little grim in the upper reaches but the start and the finish are totally wonderful. We hope that the atmosphere which emanates from the Roc d'Enfer will soon make this ride one of the classics of the area.

Start	La Moussière 930m	Duration	4 - 5 hours
Finish	La Moussière	Rating	****
Distance	17km	Terrain	****
Climb	1025m	Effort	****
Map	IGN 1:25000 3528 ET		
Access	To St Jean d'Aulps on D902 then follow signs for Grande Terche and La Moussière.		

Route

From La Moussière cycle down to the crossroads; turn right on to the road which climbs to Graydon. Cycle on to the end of the metalled road and bear left on to a wooded piste until you come to the small chalets of Graydon at 1336m. From here climb up on the left of the chapel on a path which runs through alpine pastures and reaches the ridge at 1609m (you will cycle close by the chairlifts of Chargeau and Combe de Graydon). Carry on climbing along the ridge line, and then for a time on the mountainside until you come to the arrival station of the Combe de Graydon chairlift, from where you carry on down a little way to the col de Graydon (1787m).

From the col go down along a faint track on the western side (be careful of the shifting scree) and you will come to the chalets of Grands Souvroz (1530m). From here a poorly-marked path climbs up on the right (northwards) and reaches forest cover. Continue to climb (there are some steep sectors) and cross an avalanche corridor, and then forest again until you reach the ridge line at 1659m (the col is unmarked on the IGN map). From here the chalets of Les Follys will be found below on the right. Follow the ridge line to descend rapidly to the col des Follys (1521m) and then take a sometimes rocky four wheel drive piste which will enable you to dash down to the beginning of the metalled road. Then carry on down to Moussière.

Variation

From Graydon you can carry on climbing to the top of the télécabine de Grande Terche (1490m) along the forest path. Then you can go down the piste (near the Esserailloux ski-lift) which leads back to the starting point.

Additional information

There is a pretty view from the col des Folly. When going down from Les Follys chalets look out for four wheel drives which may be coming up! Do not undertake this trip without a map and a compass.

Accommodation and food is available at 'La Moussière' gîte, courtesy of our friend, Alain.

26. SAINT JEAN D'AULPS
At the Foot of Roc d'Enfer

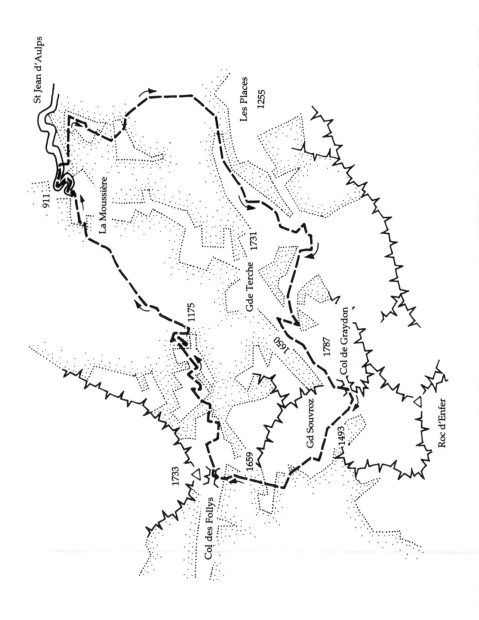

LA VALLÉE VERTE, RISSE & BREVON

Hidden beneath the first foothills which rise above the Geneva plain La Vallée Verte is a haven of greenness and tranquillity. In the Vallée Verte everything induces calm and relaxation. Far from major roads, away from tourist centres, ignored by the masses, vast alpine pastures slope gently on the mountainsides. There are wonderful views of Lake Geneva and the higher peaks in the distance.

The Vallée du Risse is a little further east. There you really feel the proximity of the high imposing summits. Between these summits and the valley are the small ranges of Brasses and Hirmentaz, and the Plaine Joux plateau which is a skier's and mountain biker's paradise.

Further north near Bioge the river Brevon flows into the Dranse as well. It rises in a narrow valley leading down from the Lac de Vallon. The lake came about in 1944 following a rock fall on the slopes below the Point de Gay. As is true of most valleys, Vallon had its own abbey of which traces remain today. Here the slopes are steeper. It is from the depths of this valley that the Roc d'Enfer rears its austere north face.

In the many forests which are found everywhere on these steep mountainsides woodcutting is very important. Lumberjacks have cut many forest paths which are ideal for mountain biking.

27. TOUR OF LA POINTE DE MIRABEL
A Trip for Families

La Pointe de Mirabel is a pretty viewpoint which you can easily climb up to on foot from Ajon. But it is equally easy to tour round this little mountain by bicycle, through welcoming countryside.

Start	Plaine Joux 1250m	Duration	1 hour
Finish	Plaine Joux	Rating	*
Distance	8km	Terrain	*
Climb	200m	Effort	*
Map	IGN 1:25000 3429 EST 3529 OUEST		
Access	On D12 through Bogève to Plaine Joux.		

Route

From the large car park follow the Ajon road and then turn left down to Fully. Turn right on the hairpin bend towards Le Replan. Continue on through Combasseran, where you come to the end of the Glappaz road, with a roundabout and a car park, at point 1205m. Then climb up to the Col de Creux and carry on to Combe (1266m). Return by climbing up to Ajon and going through Les Fangles back to the starting point.

Additional information

An easy trip on a smooth surface which is suitable for beginners or a family excursion. Café restaurants are available at Plaine Joux and Glappaz (do not forget to climb to the summit on foot).

27. TOUR OF LA POINTE DE MIRABEL
A Trip for Families

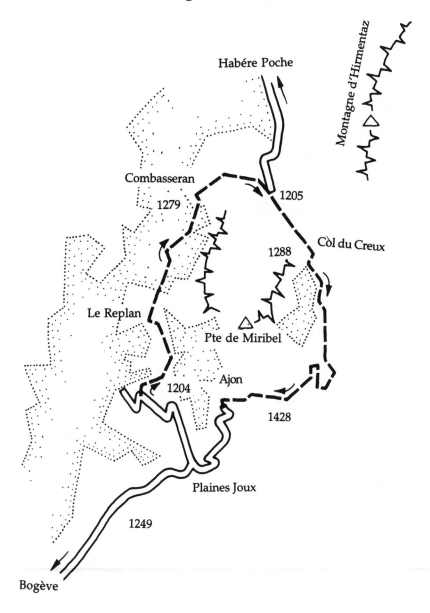

28. LA BACHAIS
In the Massif des Brasses

This is an easy ride which runs through a very peaceful area where you can get to know the small villages of Villard and Bogève.

Start	Villard 796m	Duration	1 - 2 hours
Finish	Villard	Rating	*
Distance	13km	Terrain	*
Climb	370m	Effort	**
Map	IGN 1:25000 3429 ET		
Access	From Annemasse, east on D907 to Viuz then north on D12 through Bogève to Villard.		

Route

From Villard cycle to the hamlet of Gruaz. Carry on along the path which climbs to Chez Favre, and joins the D12 which leads to the col du Perret. Turn right and climb up to Les Chaix. A path leads off into the forest and follows the ridge. It rises to a high point at 1032m and then heads down to Chez Baret and crosses the bridge which straddles the Foron river. Climb up, rejoin, and cross the D12 and return to Bogève by way of Chez Pallud, Les Trables and Les Fontaines.

Go back to the col de Perret along the road and then turn right between two small bosses (points 999m and 1005m); go down to Les Lavouets, turn left towards Chez Bouvier. Go back to Villard by way of Les Andrys.

Additional information

A good cycle path has recently been waymarked in this area.

28. LA BACHAIS
In the Massif des Brasses

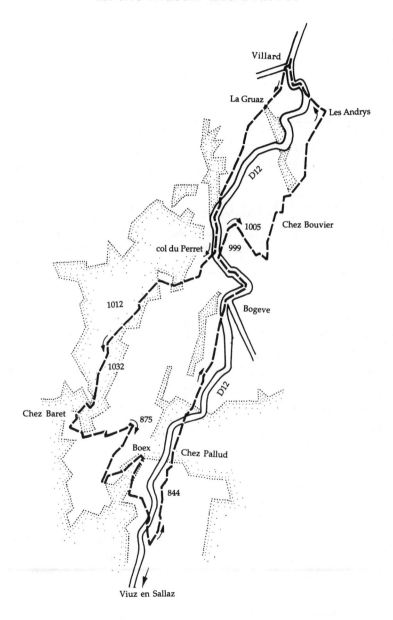

29. PÉTÉTOZ
The Lost Lake

The tiny lake of Pététoz is lost in the middle of a dense forest. The large coniferous spruce trees which surround it appear to protect it and give its waters beautiful green hues. The slopes which border it are steep and are the beginnings of the foothills of La Pointe de Chalune.

Start	La Chèvrerie 1118m	Duration	1 - 2 hours
Finish	La Chèvrerie	Rating	**
Distance	7km	Terrain	*
Climb	220m	Effort	**
Map	IGN 1:25000 3529 OUEST		
Access	From St Jeoire along the Giffre valley on D26 through Jambaz or from Bellevaux to Lac de Vallon.		

Route

From the car park at the foot of the chairlift climb up towards Plan des Rasses, but fork quickly left (point 1141m) and follow the piste which heads into the forest of Pététez a bit further on. Follow this to the end (1339m), then approach the bend at point 1333m and climb up to the lake on foot (waymarks, 100m of gradient, and 15-20 minutes climbing up).

At point 1333m, between two bends you will find a piste which passes Brevon and runs down to Les Favières and follows the right bank of the stream. It then carries on to Finge and brings you back to Chèvrerie.

Additional information

The area between Finge and Favières was really very pretty before the local town councillors decreed that the future of the parish depended on the development of a ski station, and a link with Le Grande Terche. The result of these daydreams and this muddled thinking was that the station was declared bankrupt, and the area was completely ruined.

The lake may be lost but so are our illusions ...

29. PÉTÉTOZ
The Lost Lake

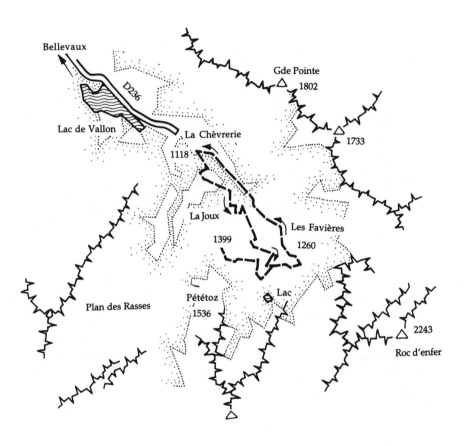

30. LA HAUTE POINTE
At the Foot of the North Face

La Haute Pointe is not all that high but it is the highest peak in the area, and its north face is very striking. It rises up steeply above the alpine pastures, strewn with fallen rocks. The forest paths of Raty and l'Arpaz which lead from Les Raches to its base offer a pleasant and varied excursion.

Start	Laitraz 870m	Duration	3 hours
Finish	Laitraz	Rating	***
Distance	15km	Terrain	*
Climb	630m	Effort	***
Map	IGN 1:25000 3529 OUEST		
Access	From St Jeoire on D26, right to D226 at Mègevette to Laitraz or from Bellevaux on D26.		

Route
Climb up towards Queuvaz and Tigny. Leave the buildings and round a bend. Carry on to join the forest path of Raty, point 1075m. Follow this road to Raty and then take the l'Arpaz piste which follows. Go through Frasseville, Rossillon and l'Arpaz and continue on to the foot of the north face of Le Haute Pointe. Leave the road and go into a field in front of a chalet (1216m).

Go down on the left of one of the paths which lead to Bieugey and on to Lapraz. Continue along the road and just before a hairpin bend on the D308 take the path which drops down to Drevy (927m). Carry on along the road back to Drevy, Asnières d'le Haut, Sométy and Laitraz.

Additional information
A beautiful ride, quite long, but not with any particular difficulties, recommended to all those who are fit.

30. LA HAUTE POINTE
At the Foot of the North Face

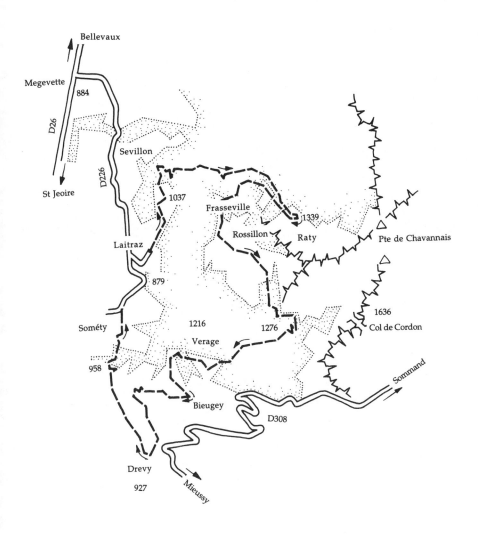

VALLEE DU GIFFRE

C ocooned in the heart of Haute-Savoie the Vallée du Giffre has many different aspects. Samoëns, the Haut-Giffre skiing centre, is protected by the Criou mountain which dominates the town, and is both the home of the master masons and of the 'Chapouets' who already have a considerable reputation. Samoëns is a holiday centre with a full range of facilities for visitors.

The valley has preserved both the charm of its ancient buildings which are grouped around the old linden tree (planted in 1432), and that of the old hamlets such as Allamands. The formidable mountain horseshoe, cirque du Fer à Cheval, is also a considerable attraction and is located east of Sixt, an attractive village with an interesting former abbey and church. If you wend your way up to this mass of rock in the very early summer the numerous waterfalls, some more powerful than others, will make an undying impression on even the most blasé of you!

The seven Samoëns mountains are also famous for the rocks of Bosseton and Criou, and the numerous chasms, of which the most famous is the Jean Bernard which is a world record depth of 1490m. But there are also numerous forests and alpine pastures to be found on both sides of the valley.

31. SAMOËNS - SIXT
Between Hamlets and Villages

This route heads from the village of Samoëns to Sixt. The small hamlets are lovely as are the two stonemason's villages. The return journey is along the main road, and the minor roads of Vallon.

Start	Samoëns 715m	Duration	1 - 2 hours
Finish	Sixt	Rating	*
Distance	11km	Terrain	*
Climb	Negligible	Effort	*
Map	IGN 1:25000 3530 EST		
Access	From Taninges on D907.		

Route

Cycle along the road from Samoëns until you come to the bridge which crosses the Clévieux torrent. Then take a right hand turn along the road which follows the left hand bank of the stream. At the end of this road, ignore the footbridge and follow the GR5-E2 which follows the Giffre river along on the left and rejoins the main road at Pernet. Cycle a little way along this road, and then cross the bridge and climb up to Faix. Carry on along the path which drops down to Giffre, and cross the stream by a footbridge. Follow the road to Sixt. Cross one of the bridges and take the D29 which heads to Hauterive and to Fay. From here go up to the Maison Neuve (828m) and you will come to Sixt.

Go back along the road as far as Soujet, then go towards the houses of Vallon d'en Haut, and Vallon d'en Bas. After this, do not join the main road but follow another small road on the right which heads to Sous la Ville. From there climb up the left bank of the Clevieux torrent and cross the Chevreret (748m). You will then soon reach the middle of the village.

Additional information

An easy trip on good roads. At Samoëns take the time to stroll in La Place du Gros Tilleul and see the alpine garden of Jaïsinia.

31. SAMOËNS - SIXT
Between Hamlets and Villages

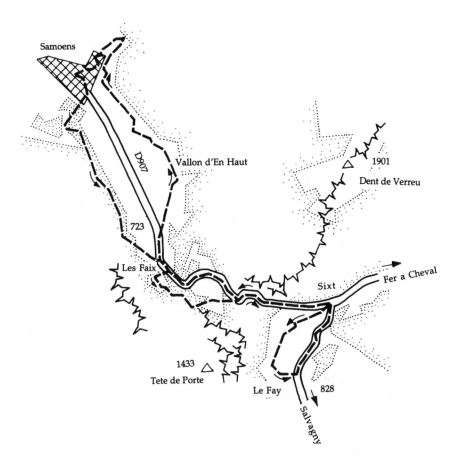

Samoens

Vallon d'En Haut

D907

1901

Dent de Verreu

723

Les Faix

Sixt

Fer a Cheval

1433

Tete de Porte

Le Fay

828

Salvagny

32. PLATEAU DE LOEX
A Gentle Family Excursion

It is suprising how certain areas remain virtually unexplored, even though they are well worth a visit. The Loex plateau is such an area. Chalet owners come and spend the weekend here and pick mushrooms or gather bilberries according to the season. The wide smooth paths which run through forests and clearings make this a great area for a family excursion or for the dilettante mountain biker.

Start	Montagne de Loex 1370m	*Duration*	1 - 2 hours
Finish	Montagne de Loex	*Rating*	*
Distance	12km	*Terrain*	*
Climb	250m	*Effort*	*
Map	IGN 1:25000 3529 OUEST & EST		
Access	From Taninges take D902 towards Les Gets. 700m after a hairpin bend turn right onto minor road towards Montagne, passing through La Biolle.		

Route

Follow the made-up road to points 1422m and 1481m. Shortly afterwards leave the Pesses road and take the next road on the right, 100m further on, and you will then come to a crossroads at 1507m. Continue along the path opposite which climbs into the forest, passing near to point 1608m, and then below the small wooded boss of Tête at 1637m, and you will come to a chalet.

Then take the path which runs down to Pré du Four (1485m) and follow a wide path which takes you back to the starting point. Then turn right to Rosière and drop down through the fields to the Mais Chalets. From there follow the forest piste which skirts Sur la Biolle and rejoins the main road at 1292m. Follow the road back to the starting point.

Additional information

The Loex plateau is a rich source of tracks and paths which are ideal for mountainbiking and offer a complete range of physical and technical challenges. With the aid of a map you can easily make up your own route from this basic circuit.

The Chapelle de Jacquicourt is marked as a ruin on the map, but this is no longer the case. It has been restored and is well worth a visit.

32. PLATEAU DE LOEX
A Gentle Family Excursion

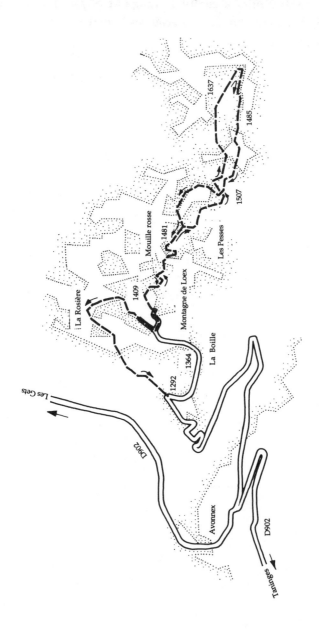

33. LAC DE GERS
The Road of Alpine Pastures

The Lac de Gers is situated at the base of a coomb of the same name, on the other side of the skiing area of Flaine; and is framed by the summits of La Tête de Véret and La Tête Pelouse. Beyond are the lapiaz of the Desert du Platé, a well known geological curiosity brought about by the snow and the trickling waters eroding the chalk. Today the Gers coomb is still used for pasture but it is also a popular area for Sunday walks.

Start	Le Béné 1150m	Duration	2 hours
Finish	Le Béné	Rating	**
Distance	14km	Terrain	**
Climb	500m	Effort	***
Map	IGN 1:25000 3530 EST		
Access	From Samoëns towards Sixt on D907 then right onto D254 towards Plateau des Saix and Le Béné.		

Route

Take the road which goes down through the forest to the Edédian bridge (1130m). Cross it and climb the steep slope which follows and heads to Roux. The metalled road continues to the chalets of Porte (1470m) crossing the streams of Grand Nant, and Nant Sec. You then follow the piste which, once out of the forest, heads to the edge of the Gers coomb, and then to the shores of the lake. You go back the same way.

Additional information

The Gers coomb, once a paradise for off piste skiers has not escaped development and high tension cables and a ski lift compete in ugliness. Even so, this trip is worth doing.

33. LAC DE GERS
The Road of Alpine Pastures

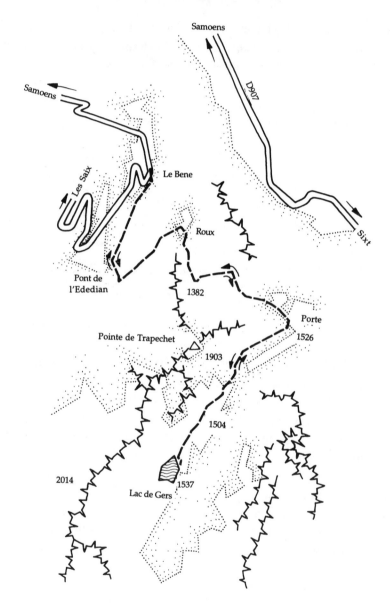

34. SIXT - FER À CHEVAL
At the Foot of Steep Rocks

At Fer à Cheval the road comes up against some impressive cliffs which overlook the forests. The mountains make you feel so small with their high steep sides as they rise up like a stark uncrossable barrier. However, in this narrow valley the banks of the Giffre offer pleasant walking country which is just as suitable for mountain biking.

Start	Sixt 760m	Duration	2 hours
Finish	Sixt	Rating	**
Distance	16km	Terrain	*
Climb	300m	Effort	*
Map	IGN 1:25000 3530 EST		
Access	From Samoëns on D907 to bridge over Giffre, just outside Sixt.		

Route
From the bridge follow the main road on the right hand bank of the Giffre. Go through l'Echarny, then Moilliet and Nantbride. Cross the stream and carry on to the next bridge (901m). Just before the bridge take the path on the left of the road which heads back to Sixt along the left bank of the Giffre. Go near Molliet (836m) and then on to Brairet, and you will reach the hamlet of Vivier, still on the same bank. Then return to Sixt and climb up to Salvagny on the D29. Cross the village and go towards the Rouget waterfall. Shortly before the Salles bridge (850m) go down the GR5-E2 between chalets and an electricity station, and then cross a stream by a footbridge and carry on down to Nants bridge. Return to Sixt on the D29.

Additional information
All the 'ups' on this trip are on minor roads, and all the 'downs' are on paths which combine to make it a very pleasant ride, suitable for all, and ideal for beginners or occasional cyclists.

Do not miss a tour of the Mason de la Réserve de Sixt which offers numerous nature based activities.

34. SIXT - FER À CHEVAL
At the Foot of Steep Rocks

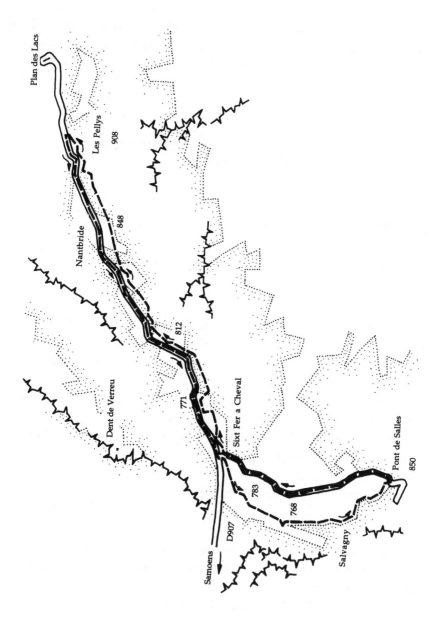

35. LES CARROZ
Going Towards Agy

A peaceful ride along the chain of hills which divide Les Carroz from the resort of Morillon. However, you will need to pedal hard to reach the high point of this trip, La Pointe de Cupoire at 1882m. From the summit there is one of those descents we love (more than 770m of height) which heads back to the centre of Carroz.

Start	Les Carroz 1109m	Duration	3 - 4 hours
Finish	Les Carroz	Rating	**
Distance	21km	Terrain	**
Climb	945m	Effort	**
Map	IGN 1:25000 3530 ET		
Access	D6 to Arâches then D106 to Carroz.		

Route

From the centre of the village take the small road which climbs from below the police station to the hamlet of Grangettes. Go past the last chalets and follow the path upwards into the forest, towards Les Sommards and on to Mottal (1411m). From there follow the path which runs straight ahead (north) and drops down to la Cantine, and Les Charmettes; and quickly reaches Agy. Then carry on along the right hand path which follows the ridge line for a while, and drops below Artoche and heads back to Mottel. From there, turn left and climb to the chalet of Biollaires, and then towards la Pointe de Cupoire.

From here it is then easy to go down to Carroz along the ridge line path. Take care in the last section near Timalets.

Additional information

Beautiful views all along this route. After Mottel this route follows the Agy skiing pistes.

35. LES CARROZ
Going Towards Agy

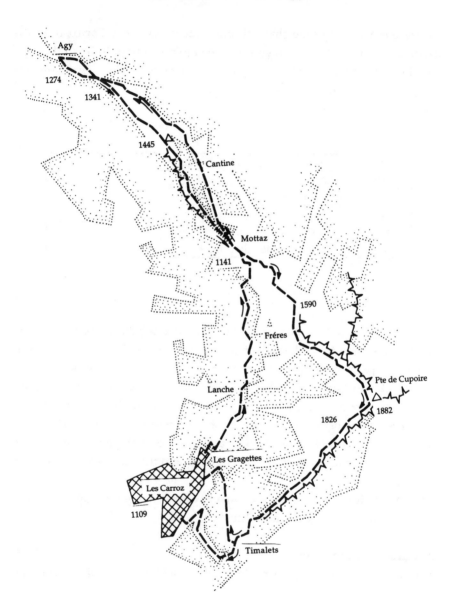

36. TOUR OF MÔLE
The Daffodil Mountain

Le Môle is so different and so distinctive that in winter its snowy summit deceives tourists seeing it from afar into mistaking it for Mont Blanc or even wondering whether it is an ancient volcano. It is very easy to understand these mistakes for its pyramid shape gives it an imposing silhouette. However, it is not that high, and it is covered with alpine fields and forests. It is also the 'daffodil' mountain, and when they bloom in the spring it becomes quite enchanting.

Start	Larsenex 908m	Duration	2 - 3 hours
Finish	Larsenex	Rating	***
Distance	11km	Terrain	***
Climb	700m	Effort	***
Map	IGN 1:25000 3429 EST		
Access	From Bonneville on D12 to Faucigny and St Jean de Tholome. Continue in direction of Bovère to Vers Château.		

Route

From Vers Château or Larsenex take the four wheel drive piste which begins in the middle of the fields. The piste then goes under the cover of trees (Saint-Jeoire forest) and rises steadily. Go through the spot heights 935m, 1065m and 1187m near the chalets of Char and carry on through the forest (high tension cable) and come out on the east face of the mountain at Granges de Cormand. From there follow the path which heads under the col de Môle (1587m) and then climb up and cross the col (a short steep passage where you will have to carry your bicycle).

On the other side of the mountain a path leads along the side and goes down to Lardère (Pêtit Môle) at 1534m. From there follow the path which drops down to Chez Béroud and on to Granges (pleasant café-restaurant) and back to the beginning.

Additional information

An excursion which has everything, with a large part of it in the forest (which is pleasant if it is hot) and a beautiful view from the col de Môle.

36. TOUR OF MÔLE
The Daffodil Mountain

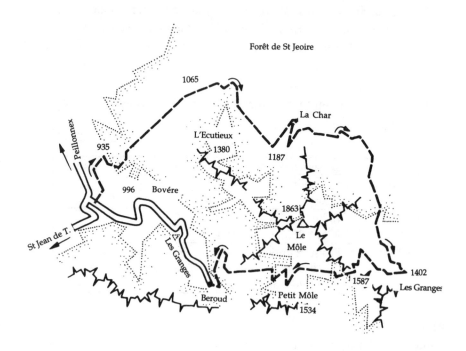

SALÈVE

The long mountain range of Salève stretches out above Genevois. It overlooks Annemasse, Geneva, and the Rhône valley which was once the bed of a gigantic glacier over 14,000 years ago. The first occupants of Salève were the Magdalanean hunters, they were followed by the Celts, and the Allobroges, and then by the Romans who left numerous traces of their occupancy.

It was as a result of his numerous ascents of Salève that the Genovese Savant Henri de Saussure decided to tackle Mont Blanc. Today Salève is mainly a place for Sunday jaunts and its high slopes are suitable for both hang and para gliding. The rocky cliff faces contrast spectacularly with the welcoming greenery of its ridges, and are a delight to local climbers.

South of Salève the areas between Roche-sur-Foron and Annecy are less dramatic and are suitable for farming and rearing animals. The whole area is well worth visiting and is criss-crossed with paths and tracks, and has numerous hamlets and villages.

Bordered on the west by Lake Annecy, Semnoz, the locals' secret garden, provides beautiful walks among the woodland. The area around Annecy is vast and there are many opportunities for mountain biking. The terrain is varied, and whether you are an expert or a beginner you will be able to find plenty of good routes.

37. LA CHAPELLE RAMBAUD - MENTHONNEX EN BORNES
Les Mottièrs

What a strange place Les Mottières is, with its craters, bosses, slopes, hedges, woods, paths, and bogs. You may well wish to extend the circuit described below and make the most of this terrain by putting all your mountain biking skills to the test.

Start	Chapelle Rambaud	Duration	1 - 2 hours
Finish	Chapelle Rambaud	Rating	*
Distance	16km	Terrain	*
Climb	250m	Effort	*
Map	IGN 1:25000 3430 OUEST		
Access	East of La Roche on D5.		

Route

From the top of the village go down the D102 and at the second bend take the right hand path which heads down through the forest and joins the D5 near Sanges. Then cycle along for about 100m on the main road and then take a minor road on the right. Next follow a path which crosses a small wood, ignore a left hand fork, and carry on to Roques.

From there go to Bellecombe and carry on to a road at spot height 851m. Then take the path opposite which heads to Bois Rond (861m). Turn left and cycle about 100m along the D102, then leave it and climb up on the right. Turn left and go below the Crêt du Merle hill. Carry on to Molety, then Chaumet (886m), crossroads of the D27 and D278. Go down the D278 towards Petit Béné and then climb to the hamlet and follow a wide path which crosses Les Mottières by the Mouille d'Arve and drop down to the hamlet of La Recule. Then turn right and go under an electric cable and climb back to point 952m (where there is a cross) and reach La Grange at 932m.

Return to Chapelle Rambaud by the road which leads to Mont Béné, then go along a path which bears left just before the hamlet, skirts the small boss of Mont Béné, drops down to the Foron torrent and climbs up by Les Chevalliers.

Additional information

This kind of route can easily by modified. You will not be able to avoid some roads but these should not prove a real pain (except to purists) and they will give beginners a chance to relax a little before beginning another off-road stretch.

37. LA CHAPELLE RAMBAUD - MENTHONNEX EN BORNES
Les Mottièrs

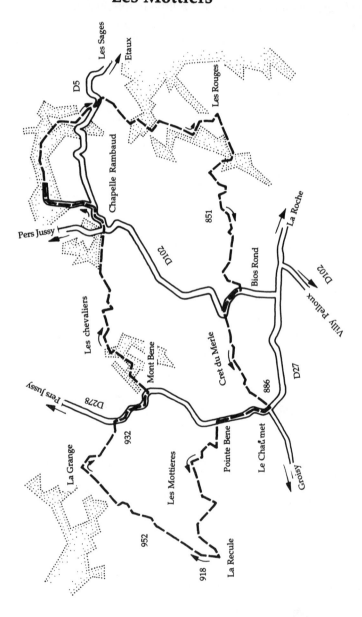

38. LE SALÈVE 1
A Visit to Trou de la Tine

The northern part of Salève is rugged; high cliffs rise above the forest giving it a somewhat austere appearance. Climbers love these cliffs and it was here in Salève that the word 'rock climbing' was invented.

Start	Ski lift station at Salève	Duration	1 - 2 hours
Finish	Salève	Rating	**
Distance	8km	Terrain	**
Climb	200m	Effort	**
Map	IGN 1:25000 3429 OUEST		
Access	From Annemasse through Mornex to Monnetier and the D41 to the Salève Téléphérique car park.		

Route

From the car park follow the road that climbs round two bends to Trés Arbres. Leave the road and go about the restaurant across the fields to Grange Passet (1133m). Follow the wide path which goes into the forest and leads to Grange Gaby (1210m), Les Rochers de Faverges, and then Pile (1230m), and rejoin the road which leads to Bouillette at 1214m. From the Bouillette crossroads climb up and round the small boss des Crêts (1278m) and cut across the fields to come to the top of Le Trou de la Tine (an opening in the rock, be careful), from where you will enjoy a fine view.

Return towards the middle of the fields where below a bend in the ridge line a faint track leads to point 1286m. Continue alongside the ridge line towards the television aerial, and then drop back down behind the Crêtes restaurant to the starting point.

Additional information

You can use the télépherique to climb to the starting point. Between 9.30-11.00 and after 17.00 bikes can be carried free of charge. At the top of the télépherique you will find a restaurant, a childrens' play area, and bicycle hire. Remember to shut all gates behind you. Le Salève does not have any drinking water so do not forget to take some with you.

38. LE SALÈVE 1
A Visit to Trou de la Tine

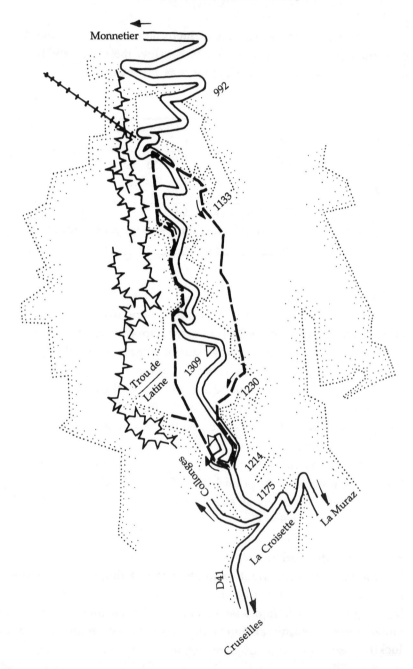

39. LE SALÈVE 2
Grand Piton, the High Point

The Grand Piton de Salève (1379m) is the high point of this ridge which overlooks the Genovese basin. The entire range is suitable for mountain biking and offers wonderful views of Annemasse, Geneva, le Jura and, in the distance, Mont Blanc.

Start	La Croisette 1175m	Duration	1 - 2 hours
Finish	La Croisette	Rating	**
Distance	12km	Terrain	**
Climb	400m	Effort	**
Map	IGN 1:25000 3429 OUEST		
Access	South from Collonges sous Salève on D45.		

Route

Leave from alongside the small téléski up a fairly steep wide path which soon reaches Le Pommier. Carry on and take the Piollière coomb to Chavanne; do not follow the ridge line but continue on its left and you will come to Chênex (1323m). Then follow the lower path which heads to the Diable cave at 1333m where there is an inn. Go along the ridgeway, D41, to Grand Piton. From there follow the road and then join the path which drops down to Thuile (1158m). Follow the wide piste, which after a long spell in the forest on the side of the mountain, goes down for some way before climbing towards the ridge.

You can easily get back to La Croisette by climbing La petite Point de la Piollière (1349m) or by retracing your steps

Additional information

While this ride is neither long nor difficult, it does involve some effort which may take beginners, or those short on training, by surprise. However, we recommend it strongly and it could be combined with ride number 38.

If you want to warm up before undertaking this circuit, you could always climb from Collonges Sous Salève up the steep road of La Croisette (good luck!).

39. LE SALÈVE 2
Grand Piton, the High Point

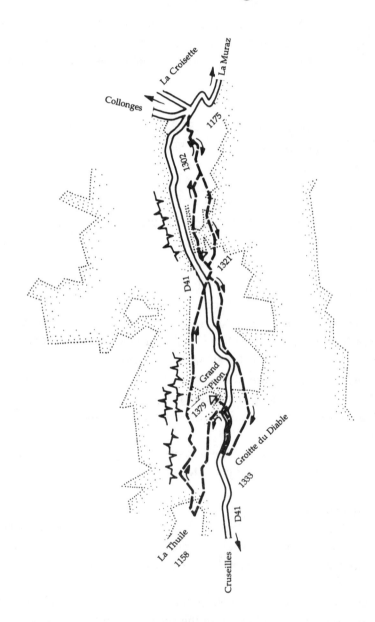

40. GROISY VILLY-LE BOUVERET
At the foot of Salève

Between Salève and le Plateau de Glières there is a lovely sunny region which offers the mountain biker suitably varied terrain, even if it is sometimes necessary to resort to metalled roads. This is yet another tour between hamlets and villages, pastures and forests, which would not be much fun to walk but is great to cycle.

Start	Leisure park at Dronières	Duration	1 - 2 hours
Finish	Dronières	Rating	**
Distance	12km	Terrain	*
Climb	450m	Effort	**
Map	IGN 1:25000 3430 OUEST		
Access	On the D27 between Menthonnex and Cruseilles.		

Route

From the leisure park at Dronières climb up a wide path behind the campsite which continues down to the village of Deyrier. Go in front of the cheese shop, cross the village, and about 300m further on, take a left hand path which passes the Usses torrent at 628m. Do not go up to Villy-le Bouveret, but almost immediately cross the Grand Verrey stream again, and climb up Le Crêt de la Biolle (a bit steep at first).

Carry on to spot height 754m a little before Mallasoire and the end of a small road. Leave this very quickly going down on the right across fields, crossing the Petit Verray stream and climbing up through the forest to reach Château Froid and Groisy. Then leave the D3, climb up between the houses on the left, follow the edge of the forest at La Mouille, and then take the D3 at spot height 804m. On leaving this road you will come to La Tour (828m) and Ferraty (793m).

Then turn right by Les Gris, and right again to drop down and cross the Grand Verray stream yet again, and climb up to Villy-le Bouveret. 250m behind the cemetery turn left and go down by Les Loverses to rejoin the route followed at the beginning and finally to return to Dronières park.

Additional information

The Dronières park is an ideal starting point where you can spend a family day out: playgrounds, picnic areas, campsites, a swimming pool and an animal park.

40. GROISY VILLY-LE BOUVERET
At the foot of Salève

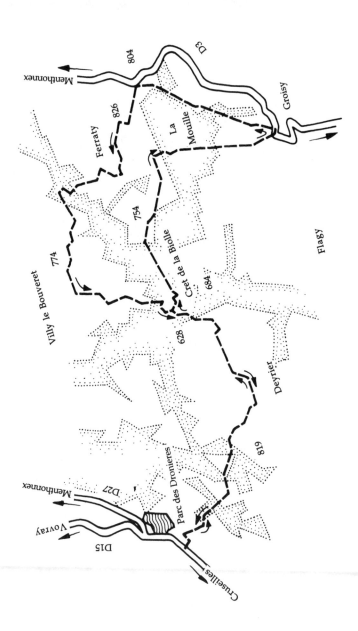

BORNES & ARAVIS

B oth these areas have become well-known, the first because of the glorious exploits which took place in these mountains during the Second World War, and the second because of the famous ski resorts such as Clusaz and Grand-Bornand, and equally because of the international reputation of the famous 'Reblochon'.

The area is dominated by mountain chains and superb unspoilt valleys, where alpine agriculture is still very much to the fore on the slopes. The Aravis mountains rise skywards in the south and the Reposoir peaks provide a natural barrier between the green and pleasant land and the Autoroute Blanche, the main route from Geneva and the west into Chamonix and Mont Blanc.

On the sporting front, as well as skiers, climbers and walkers will find challenging climbs on the Bargy mountain chain, or on the steep paths of Pointe Percée. Mountain bikers will also find many interesting routes, of great variety.

41. LES FRÈTES
An Excursion to Beauregard

La Pointe de Beauregard is the highest point on this circuit. As the name implies, it offers a wonderful view. But you do not get something for nothing, and to reach it you will need to do a good stretch of hard pedalling.

Start	Col de la Croix Fry 1467m	Duration	1 hour
Finish	Col de la Croix Fry	Rating	**
Distance	8km	Terrain	**
Climb	360m	Effort	**
Map	IGN 1:25000 3431 EST		
Access	From Thônes on D12, then on D16 towards Manigod to the col.		

Route

From the col cycle up along a good path which after a very short climb keeps to the side of the mountain, and then goes down and crosses le Nant des Prises, before climbing up towards la Pointe de Beauregard which is soon reached.

Then you go down on the west through Vaunessins before taking another path which leads to Lachat and Colomban. Shortly afterwards stop going down towards Colomban d'en Bas and take the path which climbs up to the wooded crête of the Frète mountain. Climb to the top and then ride all along the ridge before going down into the forest on the same path, and you will easily get back to the col de la Croix Fry.

Additional information

Although this is a short, fairly easy route, the ride along the ridge and the descent may cause problems to inexperienced mountainbikers. To go down safely you must beware of pedestrians and have total control of your machine. Admittedly this is a general rule but it should be borne in mind at all times.

41. LES FRÈTES
An Excursion to Beauregard

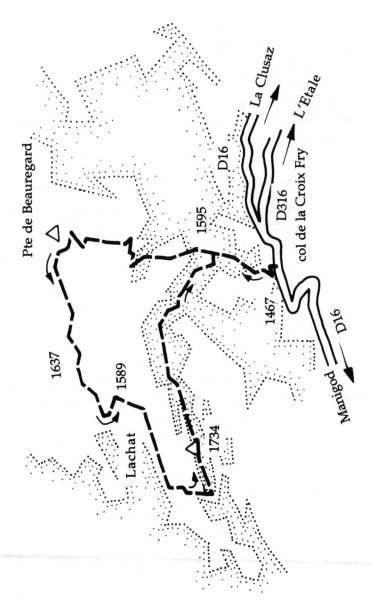

42. COL DES ANNES
At the Foot of the Queen of Aravis

The col des Annes is next to the queen of Aravis, La Pointe Percée, 2750m high and the highest point of the mountain chain of the same name. The small valley of Bouchet still houses some old chalets, examples of traditional Savoyard architecture with their slightly sloping roofs, topped with a pyramid shaped chimney, and a long hollow wooden pole which serves as a gutter. There are not many of these houses left so let us hope that they remain standing for many years to come.

Start	Grand-Bornand 923m	Duration	3 - 4 hours
Finish	Grand-Bornand	Rating	***
Distance	26km	Terrain	**
Climb	910m	Effort	***
Map	IGN 1:25000 3430 ET		
Access	From Bonneville on D12 then D224 to Grand-Bornand. From Thônes on D909 and D4.		

Route

From the centre of the village take the small road which twists round several hairpin bends to Terret, and then climbs on to Nant Robert and comes to an end at point 132m. Then follow the piste which climbs through the fields of le Grand-Montagne (1605m) carries on to Char, and adjoins a path which is suitable for motor vehicles, near the buildings of Crot. From here go down the path to the Chapelle de la Duche (1521m). Continue along the piste which climbs up to the col des Annes at 1721m.

To go back, go down on the west (following the GR96) on the side of the mountain under the Pointe de Grande Combe (you cannot really cycle on this sector - you will either have to push or carry your bike), and you will come to the chalets of Maroli d'en Haut (near the Almet ski lift). From there you can easily descent to Maroli d'en Bas (1584m) then to Bouts just above Chinaillon, and then finally by road to Grand-Bornand.

Variation

From the col des Annes it is easy to go down on the piste and then on the Plans road in the small valley of Bouchet.

Additional information

There is a mountain refuge on the col des Annes.

42. COL DES ANNES
At the Foot of the Queen of Aravis

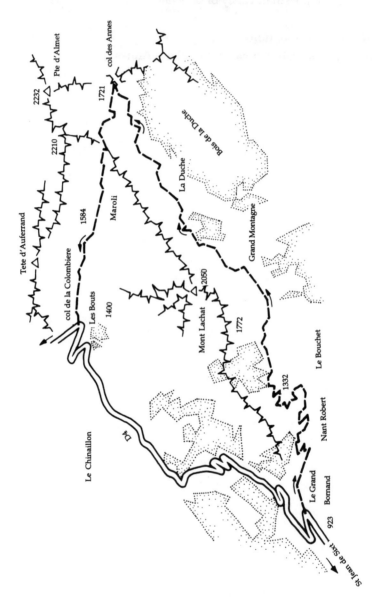

43. LAC DE LESSY
The infernal climb

Surely this climb up to the col de Forclaz which leads to the small Lessy lake must be the most difficult! You will have to be a very gifted climber to manage both the climb and the difficulties of the terrain.

Start	La Ville (Petit-Bornand) 900m	Duration	3 - 4 hours
Finish	La Ville	Rating	****
Distance	13km	Terrain	***
Climb	945m	Effort	****
Map	IGN 1:25000 3430 ET		
Access	South from Bonneville on D12 to Petit-Bornand. continue in direction of Entremont for 3km then left to La Ville.		

Route
From the end of the metalled road follow the four wheel drive piste which rises steadily under forest cover (in fact, you are following the GR96) and comes to the alpine chalets of Mayse (1476m). From there the last section which climbs up to the col de Forclaz (1844m) is the most inhuman! Continue to follow the rocky piste which leads to the col. If you actually reach the col a gentle descent will take you to the lake and the Lessy chalets at 1750m.

Retrace your steps on the return journey, but be very careful for the piste is extremely steep.

Additional information
There are two café-bars on this journey, one at the Mayse chalets, and one at the Lessy chalets.

Food and accommodation are available at the gîte Le Marsolan in the hamlet at Ville.

43.   LAC DE LESSY
The infernal climb

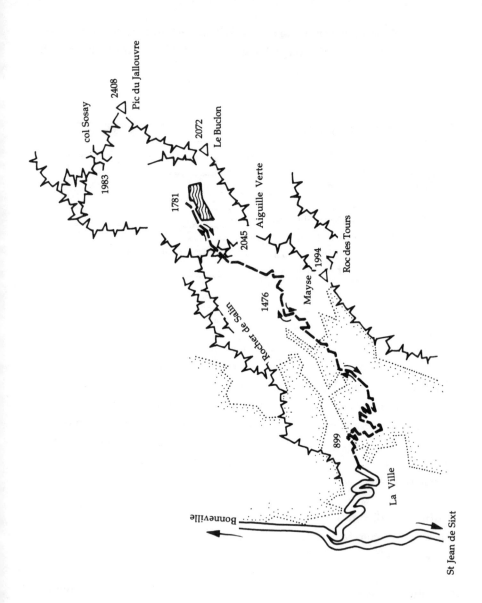

44. PETIT-BORNAND
By Le Pas du Loup

A beautiful alpine excursion at one of the high spots of local contemporary history, Le Plateau des Glières. For it was here in January 1944 that more than 450 maquisards staved off the attack of the Milice de Vichy and alpine Nazi troops, who were much more numerous and better equipped. The withdrawal took place on 26th March 1944 after heavy fighting.

Start	Petit-Bornand 728m	Duration	4 - 5 hours
Finish	Petit-Bornand	Rating	****
Distance	33km	Terrain	**
Climb	1150m	Effort	****
Map	IGN 1:25000 3430 ET		
Access	South from Bonneville on D12 to Petit-Bornand. The start point is1.5 km on the right after the village, at a minor road for l'Essert Plateau.		

Route

Take the minor road which climbs to Talavé, carry on along the four wheel drive piste to Glières, and reach the plain by the large chalet of Chez la Jode. Then turn left towards the monument and the col de Glières at 1425m. From here drop down on the left of the path which goes through Vers le Creux and heads to Paccot. Go down towards the memorial, on towards Les Pâres and then climb up on a forest road to the Plaine de Dran.

Cross the plain on the east, go through Côte Fierdet and reach the two groups of chalets (not named on the map) at 1540m and 1601m. A steep climb from the last chalet will take you up to the Pas du Loup (1800m) and then you can go swiftly down to the chalets of Auges at 1755m. From there a long downhill sector leads to a small metalled road at Malvoisin (940m). Carry on down to the village of Entremont, and return along the D12 to the starting point.

Additional information

Once you have climbed up there are wonderful views over the Pas du Loup and Auges mountain.

There is a spectacular descent from the chalets of Auges to Entremont, with a drop of 984m.

44. PETIT-BORNAND
By Le Pas du Loup

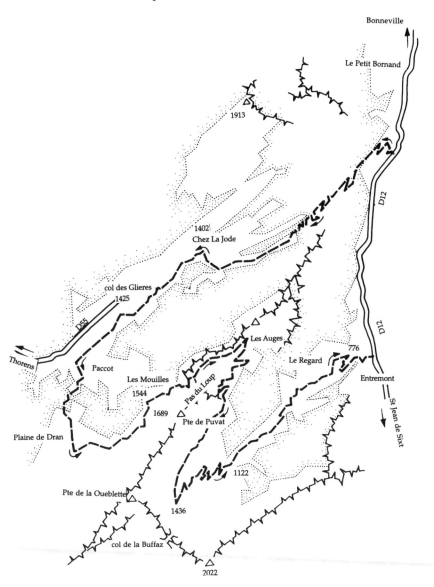

Bonneville

Le Petit Bornand

D12

1913

1402
Chez La Jode

col des Glieres
1425

D55

Thorens

Les Auges

Le Regard

776

D12

Entremont

St Jean de Sixt

Paccot

Les Mouilles
1544

Pas du Loup

1689

Pte de Puvat

Plaine de Dran

1122

Pte de la Oueblette

1436

col de la Buffaz

2022

MONT BLANC

This vast mountainous area notably includes the Val d'Arly with Megève, and le Val Montjoie, the standard bearer of the valley, the thousand-year-old Saint Nicholas-de-Véroce. The prestigious valley of Chamonix also contains theContamines, Servoz and the Diosaz gorges and is dominated by the alpine chain of Haute-Savoie with the splendour of Mont Blanc towering above everything.

If the area's international reknown is due mainly to the winter sports facilities, the Mont Blanc countryside can justifiably be proud of its three nature reserves; the Contamines reserve, the Passy reserve and the Aiguilles Rouges reserve. All three have very varied flora and fauna (chamois, ibex, mermots, grouse).

All the rides in this section will please both those high altitude fanatics who like nothing better than to haul their bikes up above the snow line, and those who like to pause and reflect and study the small hamlets which reveal the true character of the area. What a place to go mountain biking, with the sun glinting on the snow clad peaks and intoxicating alpine air.

45. CHAMONIX - BOIS DU BOUCHET
At the Foot of the Needles

The needles, the high summits, and the glaciers of the massif of Mont Blanc totally surround Chamonix.

The world capital of alpine sports is not really the best place for mountain biking, because the extremely steep slopes are not suitable for 'normal' bikes and require expert skills. However, the bottom of the valley offers some possibilities.

Start	Chamonix 1030m	Duration	2 hours
Finish	Chamonix	Rating	*
Distance	15km	Terrain	*
Climb	200m	Effort	*
Map	IGN 1:25000 3630 OT		
Access	Autoroute Blanche to Chamonix.		

Route

Take the N505 road towards Les Praz from the roundabout as you come into Chamonix. After about 500m turn left in front of the forest house and cycle into the Bouchet wood. Follow the path which bears right and crosses the wood. It leads back to the road which you cross and then take the wide path opposite, keeping on the left bank of l'Arveyron. The path climbs slightly and goes under the EDF télépherique.

Shortly afterwards leave this path on a hairpin bend and go down to the flood plain. Then go back below the EDF télépherique and cross the Himalayan bridge. From here turn immediately right and go under the EDF télépherique again, and follow the right hand bank of the stream for a little way. A path continues on the Piget slope, drops down in the forest and comes out at the hamlet of Gaudenays. From there go back to the road at Les Praz and return to Chamonix through the Bouchet wood.

Additional information

The paths on this route are very smooth; you should be careful of the numerous walkers who like to stroll in the Bouchet wood. You could indeed visit the Chamonix alpine museum.

45. CHAMONIX - BOIS DU BOUCHET
At the Foot of the Needles

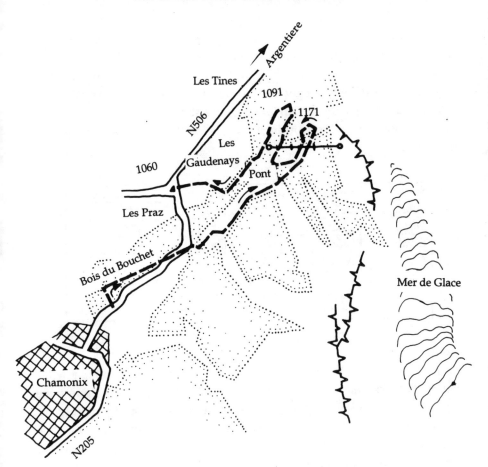

46. LE BETTEX
Between Val Montjoie and Val d'Arly

A pretty, varied circuit with an amazing backdrop. Le Mont d'Arbois in the south, Christomet in the west, the massif of Mont Blanc in the east, and the vallée de l'Arve in the north. This ride is also a good opportunity for a beginner to learn how to negotiate slopes and descents by undertanding the profile and nature of the terrain (braking on a slippery surface, approaching a boss, jumps, etc) and by learning how to select the right speed and gear at the right time.

Start	Le Bettex 1440m	Duration	2 hours
Finish	Le Bettex	Rating	**
Distance	11km	Terrain	**
Climb	570m	Effort	**
Map	IGN 1:25000 3531 OT		
Access	From Saint-Gervais on D909, in direction of Megève, and at the Robinson Sawmill turn right onto the D43 and D343 to Bettex.		

Route

From Bettex follow the piste (on the right of the télépherique for a while below the small téléski) which climbs up to l'Avenaz (1625m). From there leave the piste and follow the path which drops down on the right to the houses of Propacot (1490m). You carry on down across fields to a junction where you turn left under forest cover. Carry on down a good slope to the large building of Combafort (1200m). Turn left and take the path which joins the Vers le Nant road. When you reach the road turn left.

At Vers le Nant stop climbing and follow a small road on the left which runs between the two houses of Plan. The road becomes a track and leads to a junction where you turn right up to Prapacot. Just before Prapacot turn left and drop down in the forests to the place named Plan Genêts (1256m). Follow the right hand path which goes towards Planset, and then carry on along a path, which, on emerging from the woods, comes out at a house.

After the house, climb up on the right and carry on across the fields (go under the Monts Rossets chairlift) towards Bettex, where you will come to a rocky piste just before the village.

Additional information
The various forest sectors will demand strength and skill to cross obstacles such as tree stumps and roots.

46. LE BETTEX
Between Val Montjoie and Val d'Arly

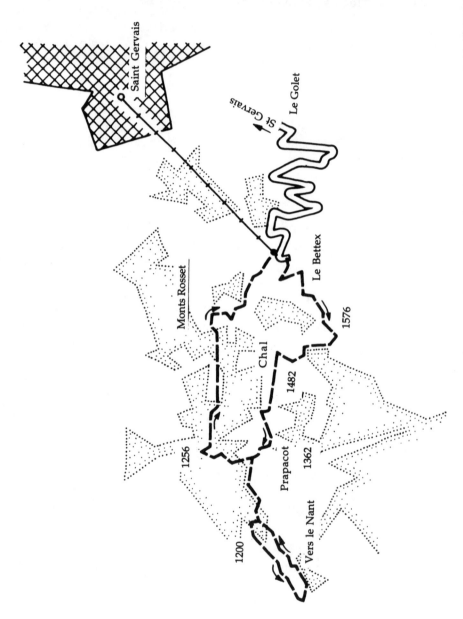

47. COL DE VOZA
At the Foot of Mont Blanc

This ride which runs through the col de Voza and the col de la Forclaz must be one of the most attractive both because of the beauty and majesty of the countryside, and the special atmosphere which you feel high up in the mountains.

Start	Bionnay 952m	Duration	4 hours
Finish	Bionnay	Rating	***
Distance	22km	Terrain	****
Climb	1100m	Effort	****
Map	IGN 1:25000 3531 ET		
Access	From le Fayet go south on D902 through St Gervais to Bionnay.		

Route

From the small town of Bionnay climb up the road to Bionnassay. Leave the hamlet and go towards Crozat (a steep climb will lead you through Sur le Cart and Fioux) and bring you to the col de Voza at 1653m. From here carry on through Delevret to the Prarion hostel where you can stop for a welcome snack!

Go down the same way under the Prarion ski lift and take the right hand path which leads to Charme (1799m) firstly through forest and then through fields. This path quickly loses height and there is a spectacular descent which runs down through Cha (ignore the path on the right which leads to the Chalet des Anglais) and comes out at Combettes. From here the forest piste climbs under the cool trees to the col de Forclaz (1533m).

Go down on the western path which goes through le Pontet (1376m) and Montfort (1181m) and ends at Toilles (the descent from the col to Montfort is pretty sensational!). Then return to Saint-Gervais and Bionnay along the main road.

Variation

From the col de Voza you can climb along the Mont Blanc tramway lines to la Chalette (1801m), the arrival station of the Houches télépherique. You could do a section of this route from Houches by going up on the Prarion cable car.

Additional information

Water is available at Pontets. The more cowardly among you, or downhill fanatics, could drive up to Bionnasay in a car and then take the TMB (Mont Blanc tramway) to Chablette. Because of the steep descents which will place your tyres and brakes under considerable pressure, make sure that your bike is in good condition before setting out on this circuit!

47. COL DE VOZA
At the Foot of Mont Blanc

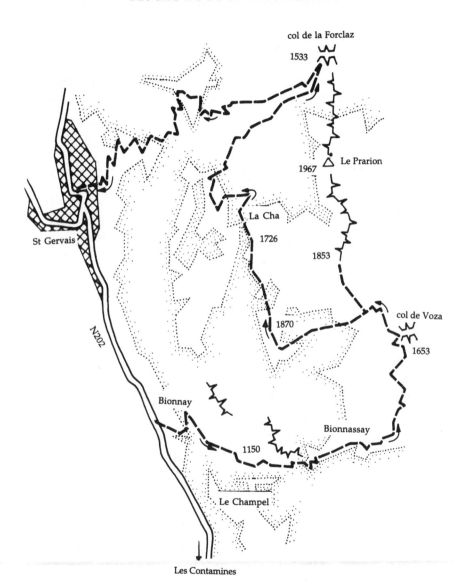

col de la Forclaz

1533

Le Prarion

1967

La Cha

1726

1853

St Gervais

col de Voza

1653

N202

1870

Bionnay

Bionnassay

1150

Le Champel

Les Contamines

48. BIONNASSAY
Under the Vorassay Rocks

This very pretty circuit will enable you to discover the charming valley of Bionnassay, which is found at the foot of the glacier of the same name. The climb from Bionnay can surprise even the bravest but it is a necessary prelude to the speedy, difficult descent which will enable you to push yourself to your limits.

Start	Bionnay 952m	Duration	2 hours
Finish	Bionnay	Rating	***
Distance	10km	Terrain	***
Climb	455m	Effort	***
Map	IGN 1:25000 3531 ET		
Access	From le Fayet go south on D902 through St Gervais to Bionnay.		

Route

From Bionnay a good stiff climb brings you to the charming hamlet of Bionnassay (1320m). Carry on to Crozat and take the right hand path which runs between the chalets and leads to Maisonnette. Then go down on the right to the Pont des Places (1413m) which straddles the cold waters coming straight from the nearby Bionnossay glacier. From the bridge climb up a little way below the Chalère chalet and take the right hand path which drops down through l'Ormey and the chalet of Presbert to the hamlet of Champel. Then cross the hamlet and turn left on a wide bend on to a path which leads down to la Villette (take care!).

Turn right and follow the path which joins the Contamines road and the bridge of Bon Nant. Take the road towards Saint-Gervais for about 200m and then turn right on the path which leads back to Bionnay.

Additional information

There are lots of great photo-opportunities, do not forget your camera. Food is available at both the Bionnassay and Champel inns.

48. BIONNASSAY
Under the Vorassay Rocks

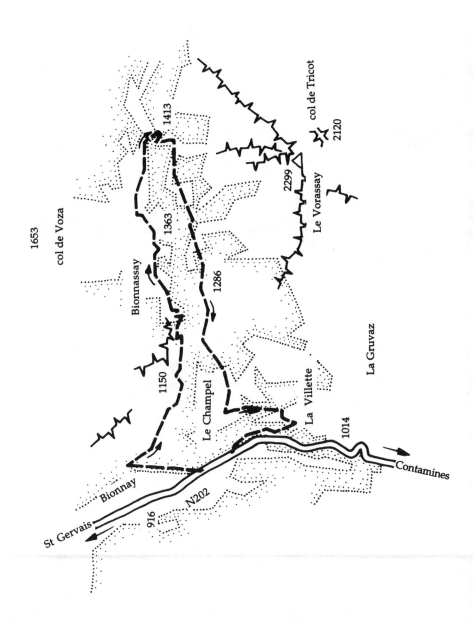

49. CHALET DE MAYÉRES
Windward to the Quatre Têtes

The Mayéres chalet is situated at the foot of the Quatre Têtes, on the east side of Aravis which rises above Sallanches and the valley of l'Arve opposite the Mont Blanc chain. From there the view all around is varied, and the ride interesting, but physically demanding.

Start	Bursier 970m	Duration	2 - 3 hours
Finish	Bursier	Rating	***
Distance	10km	Terrain	***
Climb	600m	Effort	***
Map	IGN 1:25000 3430 ET		
Access	From Sallanches climb to the end of the Doran road.		

Route

From the car park take the four wheel drive path which climbs steeply to the Doran chalets (signposted). Just after the Planes chalets carry on along left on the four wheel drive piste which climbs to the Mayères mountain refuge. You will find it easily but you will have to do some hard pedalling to actually reach the refuge.

To return, follow the path down past the chalet of Aiguilles (1524m) to Marcolez, and then on to Grange Ville and you will then reach Couterre after a short stretch in the forest. From there it is easy to carry on down to Grand Essert where you will come to the metalled road. Follow this through the hamlet of Houches to return to where you started.

Additional information

Food and shelter are available at the Mayères mountain refuge. If you are lucky you may meet the owner Raymond Martinette, a jolly mountain dweller, a former ski jumping champion, a poet and author, unstoppable on the topic of his mountains and his locality, who would be delighted to inscribe a copy of his book for you 'Au Vent des Quatre Têtes'.

49. CHALET DE MAYÉRES
Windward to the Quatre Têtes

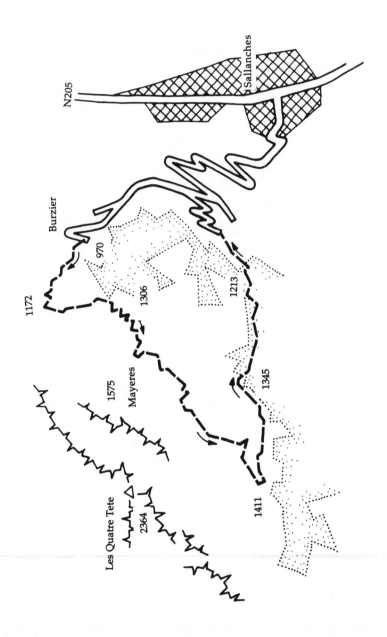

50. LAC DE PORMENAZ
In a Green Jewel Case

The Lac de Pormenaz, situated at nearly 2000m, is a true mountain lake and makes a great finishing point to a ride. The good four wheel drive piste which climbs to the Moëde Anterne mountain refuge, and comprises the main part of this trip, makes for particularly good cycling. However, the considerable drop and the sheer length of this circuit mean that you need to be experienced.

Start	Plaine Joux 1337m	Duration	2 - 3 hours
Finish	Plaine Joux	Rating	***
Distance	18km	Terrain	**
Climb	630m	Effort	**
Map	IGN 1:25000 3530 ET		
Access	From Sallanches take the D13 at Passy, over the plateau and east to Plaine Joux.		

Route

Ignore the Lac Vert road which runs downwards and take the higher road which climbs above the chalets. This road soon gives way to a four wheel drive piste which goes through Chatelet (1418m) continues towards Ayères and climbs up to the impressive rock face of Fiz, near the Rocher du Marteau. The path continues below this long and imposing barrier and leads to the mountain refuge of Moëde Anterne at 2002m. Follow the path which drops down to the bridge at Arlevé (GR5) for a very short way and then leave it to go to Laouchet, and then to the Lac de Pormenaz along the waymarked road (1945m).

To go down, simply retrace your steps.

Additional information

The views from Plateau d'Assy all along the Mont Blanc chain are quite outstanding.

Food and accommodation are available at the Moëde Anterne mountain refuge. This ride runs through the Passy nature reserve.

50. LAC DE PORMENAZ
In a Green Jewel Case

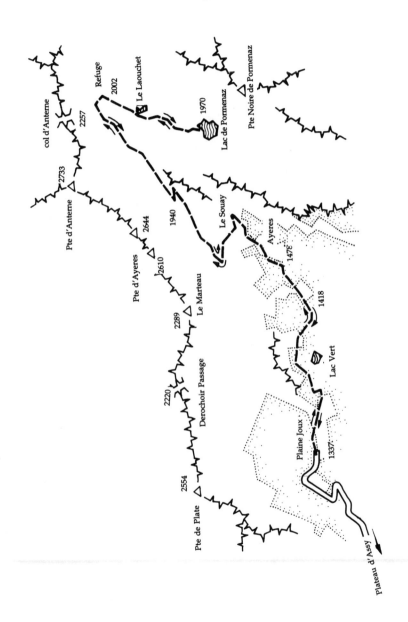

- NOTES -

- NOTES -

- NOTES -

TWO WHEELS

BREATHING SPACES - Bike Rides Within Easy Reach of London - Patrick Field.

24 bike rides, easily reached from London by car or by train. A great mix of on and off-road routes, all day rides for mountain bikers and tourers, leisurely country lanes and family rides. With route maps, details of places to see and refreshment stops. *Pbk, 170pp, £7.99.*

Cox's Rural Rides - 36 tours in the south-east - Tim Cox.

The choice of tours ranges from short excursions to challenging day trips - routes can easily be linked to form longer routes. The illustrated descriptions include details of places to see, fascinating local history and where to stop for food and drink. *Pbk, 272pp, £8.99.*

COUNTY RIDES - Thirty Rides in Thirteen Counties - Simon Shaw & Anna Pond - Bike 1.

This collection of 30 rides will allow all cyclists to explore the glory of the English countryside - from beginners looking for a leisurely ride in the country to dedicated enthusiasts searching for mileage. With detailed maps and easy to follow directions. *Pbk, 168pp, April 1994, £8.99.*

GET LOST - Off-Road Adventures With A Bicycle Within Easy Reach Of London - Patrick Field.

An off-road follow up to Breathing Spaces, packed with great escapes from London and the suburbs to the countryside. *Pbk, 192pp, £7.99.*

Available from all good bookshops or direct from the publisher plus £1 postage & packing per copy. Two Heads Publishing, 12A Franklyn Suite, The Priory, Haywards Heath, West Sussex, RH16 3LB.

TWO WHEELS

BREATHING SPACES - Bike Rides Within Easy Reach of London - Patrick Field.

24 bike rides, easily reached from London by car or by train. A great mix of on and off-road routes, all day rides for mountain bikers and tourers, leisurely country lanes and family rides. With route maps, details of places to see and refreshment stops. *Pbk, 170pp, £7.99.*

Cox's Rural Rides - 36 tours in the south-east - Tim Cox.

The choice of tours ranges from short excursions to challenging day trips - routes can easily be linked to form longer routes. The illustrated descriptions include details of places to see, fascinating local history and where to stop for food and drink. *Pbk, 272pp, £8.99.*

COUNTY RIDES - Thirty Rides in Thirteen Counties - Simon Shaw & Anna Pond - Bike 1.

This collection of 30 rides will allow all cyclists to explore the glory of the English countryside - from beginners looking for a leisurely ride in the country to dedicated enthusiasts searching for mileage. With detailed maps and easy to follow directions. *Pbk, 168pp, April 1994, £8.99.*

GET LOST - Off-Road Adventures With A Bicycle Within Easy Reach Of London - Patrick Field.

An off-road follow up to Breathing Spaces, packed with great escapes from London and the suburbs to the countryside. *Pbk, 192pp, £7.99.*

Available from all good bookshops or direct from the publisher plus £1 postage & packing per copy. Two Heads Publishing, 12A Franklyn Suite, The Priory, Haywards Heath, West Sussex, RH16 3LB.